From Victi

Publishing Company
Xcellence Publications LLC
P.O. Box 181023 Cleveland, OH 44112

Courtney N. Hauser

From Victim
to Survivor

Publishing Company
Xcellence Publications LLC
P.O. Box 181023 Cleveland, OH 44118

sur•vi•vor

noun

a person who survives, especially a person remaining alive after an event in which others have died.
"the sole survivor of the massacre"

a person who copes well with difficulties in their life.
"she is a born survivor"

This book is dedicated to my mother, Cie Dale.
She is the epitome of a sur-viv-or.

From Victim to Survivor

Dear Friend,

I'm sorry for everything that you have experienced. I know that it hurts, and you certainly didn't deserve it. Yes, they should have protected you, believed you and defended you. They should have fought for you instead of turning their backs. I'm sorry that you were abandoned, betrayed and manipulated. I'm sorry for every black eye and busted lip, and the pain you experienced. I know you trusted them and you gave them all you had. I know that in return you got nothing but sleepless nights, headaches and tears. I'm sorry that your parents weren't there like they were supposed to be. My heart hurts knowing that you didn't get the love you needed from them. I'm sure you've started to think that your life experiences are a reflection of who you are. You probably think you're not good enough, undeserving of love, ugly or damaged. You may feel worthless, hopeless or extreme sadness. And so you retreat. You isolate. You remove yourself from anyone and everyone that might be able to hurt or help you. Maybe you cut your wrists, take an extra sleeping pill at night or secretly wish you were dead. These feelings and thoughts have probably been around for a long time, and it seems as if they just won't go away. But I want you to know that there is hope and help. As you read this book I challenge you to serve an eviction notice to the victim that may live inside of you. The victim that blames you for what you experienced even if it wasn't your fault. The victim that causes you to sink into darkness and question your identity. It has taken up your energy, your sanity and your peace long enough, and now it's time for it to go! You were created with the ability to survive. To carry on despite hardships or trauma, to cope, to remain functional or usable, to live, persist and persevere after a setback. I encourage you to keep going despite pain, discomfort or less than desirable circumstances. You were designed to fight, to push past and overcome. Each chapter in this book details my experiences as a Victim. But my story doesn't end there—and yours doesn't either. At the end of each chapter you'll find survival tips. Things I wish I knew back then or things I wish someone would have told me. Tips I used later in life to transition from a Victim to Survivor. I survived the issues of life, and you can too. I hope you find yourself somewhere in these pages and that the Survivor in you comes alive!

Sincerely,
A Survivor

Courtney N. Hauser, LPC

Contents

Surviving...

From Victim to Survivor

ONE

Against the Odds

It's a Girl

December 25, 1990 my mother was at the table eating Christmas dinner when suddenly her water broke. This was her third pregnancy so she was no stranger to childbearing. She continued to eat and said, "I'll go to the hospital when I finish my food!" My grandmother's southern-style, everything made from scratch cooking must have been that good. As December 26 rolled around, my mother pushed out a 6lbs 10oz fair skinned, slanted eyes, curly haired baby. I was the only daughter of Cynthia Elaine, and the baby girl of Leon Malone Sr. My parents decided to take their nicknames Lee and Cie and put them together to form the name Leecy (pronounced Lee-C). The story goes that my mother didn't care much for this name, but when the nurse asked what my name was my father proudly pronounced "Leecy". My mother had pondered over other names like Cinnamon, Lelani and Waverly. She later decided that as her only girl she wanted my name to begin with a C like her own. Eventually she renamed me Courtney Noel Malone. I must have been a smart kid because somehow I was able to figure out that my name was no longer Leecy and responded to the name Courtney when called.

My mother gave all of her children names that had significant meaning to her. She was a woman who loved to learn about other cultures and languages. The French language and culture was her favorite. This is where the name Noel came from. It's my father's name spelled backwards and it means Christmas in French. Seeing that I arrived shortly after Christmas, the name Noel seemed to fit me well. My mother figured it was only right to give her baby girl a name from the language she loved. I was my mother's third child and my father's seventh. Two years later my mother had my baby brother and brought my father's total count to 8 children. He had 4 children prior to meeting my mom; Troy, Tilisha, Avian and Leena, who all had different mothers. He then had his final four children with my mother; Leon Jr (Lee), Lance (Lem), Myself and Lorean (Lou).

My mother Cynthia, now known as Cie, was the creative type. She loved to read, dance, write, and learn about other cultures and languages. She even had a poem she wrote, which was published in a book. She was loving, kind and had a smile that could light up a whole room. Her approach to parenting was helping us discover our creative niche and encouraging us to grow in our talents.

In our toddler years, my mother skipped out on all the goo goo gagas and began speaking and teaching us real words. All four of us were able to walk and talk at an early age. As we grew older we had to learn slang from our friends and other family members because it was never spoken in our house. Proper speech was ingrained in us so much so that my family frequently tells the story about a conversation I had with my cousin and aunt at 2 years old. We were shopping in the Golden Gate plaza looking for household items. My cousin Carolyn who was 12 years old at the time gladly pushed me along in the shopping cart. She said to me, "You know Coco Chanel (my nickname then), I can't wait until you get older. You gone be my road dog and I'm not gonna let nothing happen to you. If somebody gets in your face, you betta get in theirs and tell them, I AIN'T the ONE!" I responded back by saying, "You mean I AM NOT the one?" No, Carolyn said, "I mean I AIN'T the one!" I then offered her a contraction to use in the phrase, "How about I'M not the one?" Carolyn yelled for her mom, my Aunt Regina, and said, "Mama, tell Courtney you can't have an attitude and be all proper with it!" My Aunt replied, "Well yes you can, you just have to say it like you mean it. Like this…": She leaned in close to me, put her hand on her hip and said I'M NOT THE ONE." I leaned up in the cart towards the handlebar, twisted my neck and said I'M NOT

EITHER!" My auntie leaned back and said, "Okaaayyy, I think she has it!" Lo

My sassiness was definitely a trait passed down from my Aunt Regina and Cousin Carolyn. My mother was sassy too but with much less attitude. As my personality began to blossom, my mother discovered two talents I naturally possessed: creativity and intelligence. At 4 years old I begged my mother to go to school. She told me I was too young and had to wait until I turned 5. I continued to stay persistent and my mother felt that I was prepared to go to school with the big kids. She took me downtown for testing to see if I could test into kindergarten and guess what happened!? This girl passed with flying colors! I began elementary school at age 4. I loved learning, drawing, reading, writing and dancing. I took on my mother's love for culture and began learning to speak French at 4 years old. I asked her about our own culture and would enjoy trips with her to the Native American Festival.

For years I wanted to be Kristi Yamaguchi, the famous professional figure skater. How many little black girls do you know that want to be an Asian figure skater? My mom never made race an issue and encouraged me to be whatever I wanted. When I turned 5 my mother and I began taking a dance class at Cleveland State University called "Saturday in the Studio." We learned everything from African Dance, to Jazz, Swing dancing, and R&B. I was even given the opportunity to perform in a concert at Caine Park with the College Dance Students. My mother and I performed mother/daughter dances and we looked forward to every Saturday. She was my mommy and I was her mini me.

As I grew older, I really began to admire my mother. She was a single mother of 4 who worked tirelessly to make sure we had everything we needed. She and my father had divorced and we were pretty much on our own. My mother taught us to be very independent and to take care of one another. When my brother Lance was 10, he had the responsibility of getting me and my little brother Lou up in the morning, getting us ready, making sure we ate breakfast and walking us 12 streets over to the elementary school. Lance was certainly a drill sergeant and didn't take any slack from me and Lou.

There's a funny story about Lance and his drill sergeant days. On one occasion he was getting us ready for school like he normally did; this particular day I seemed to be taking a little longer than usual. Lance said to me, "Come on, hurry up we've got to get to school on time." He did not believe in being late to school; apparently I did. I yelled back at him, "You're not the boss of me!" My sassiness decided it was time to make another debut. Lance shot back, "If you don't hurry up I'm going to leave you because I can't be late." I responded, "I don't care go ahead." I assumed that he was bluffing and wouldn't leave his 8 year old sister home alone. Welp he wasn't bluffing! Lance walked straight out that door and left me home alone! He was not going to let anything get in the way of being late to school; not even his baby sister! I called my mother and removed all the sass in my voice that I had just given my brother. Instead, I was crying and telling my mom how Lance had "left me." I guess he showed me. That never happened again. My attitude went into hiding—well at least with Lance it did!

The four of us stayed with my mother because my father had chosen the path of drugs, domestic violence and stealing. I believe he loved us yet left to pursue his first love at the time: drugs. My parents divorced when I was very young and I actually don't even remember us all living together as a family. After the divorce, my father moved in with my grandmother and we spent weekends and vacations at their house. My father wasn't around much but my grandmother was always there for us. She was a fair skinned, short, curvy woman who touched the hearts of so many. Everyone loved my grandmother. I'm talking the entire neighborhood around 144th in Kinsman and Bartlett. Everyone called her grandma. We called her grandma sugarlump because she was so sweet. My grandma was the kind of person that never said no to anyone. This was good for us kids but often times adults (family members included) would take advantage of her because she was so nice.

Grandma always favored the boys more than she did the girls. Lou in particular was her baby. You could pretty much do whatever you wanted at grandma's house as long as you didn't mess with her baby. If you got on her nerves she would say "Don't make me show my color!" Summers at grandma's were the best. All the kids on the street would try their best to fit on grandma's small 3-step porch. We would all fight over who was going to sit in that one chair on the porch. I don't know why we never bought more chairs. We had the smallest porch on the street yet it was always covered by the most kids. Every weekend grandma would take us shopping and out to Bob Evans. Often times there were so many kids at her house she would have to take us in groups. The boys would go first of course and then when they came back it was the girl's turn.

I bet you're wondering how grandma had so much money. She was a teacher in the East Cleveland School District, but she never spent her money on herself. She lived in a not so great neighborhood and drove an average car so that she could put all her money into her family. Grandma owned 3 houses and family members stayed in all her properties. She managed her money well so that we never went without. Grandma knew that the men in her family didn't do such a great job financially taking care of their children. So for some reason, she gladly picked up the slack.

Since my other siblings were older and had different mothers, we didn't spend much time with them. Troy was already an adult and had a family of his own in Columbus. He came into town every so often and boy did I love when he did. I was his baby sister so he always made sure I felt loved and special. He would pick me up and swing me around and tell me how pretty I was. Leena lived with her mom, but also stayed with my grandmother for awhile, so we got a chance to see her on the weekends and during the summer. It wasn't until years later that we met Avian and Tilisha.

So far my life sounds pretty good right? Yeah my parents split early on, but I had a great relationship with my mom, my brothers and my grandmother helped out tremendously. So what was the problem? What I didn't mention in my recap of the early years was that I was set up to FAIL…yes you read correctly, I was set up to FAIL.

Destination…Failure

See, before I even had a chance at life, rape, incest, drug addictions, domestic violence, abuse, suicide, mental health issues and poverty flowed through my bloodlines. These were the family secrets that no one wanted to talk about because if you grew up like I grew up then you knew that "What goes on in this house, stays in this house." It was ingrained in us as little children; an unwritten rule passed down throughout several generations. If I had to guess, I would say it probably took its origins in the black community during slavery in which it was crucial that what happened and what was discussed among slaves needed to stay among slaves for their safety and protection. Even after slavery this mentality proved to be necessary among black families to foster safety and protection against government authorities. In essence the 'What goes on in this house stays in the house" mentality was supposed to mean that whatever problems we had in the family we could take care of them on our own. It suggested that we didn't need anyone outside our family i.e. social workers, counselors or teachers to help us resolve our issues. In fact, many children in black households were told that we better not bring those "nosy white people" into our business or there would be consequences and repercussions. Sound familiar?

At one point this mentality served its purpose but it also left some questions unanswered. What if the people in the house were the cause of the problems? What if the people in the house couldn't help resolve the problem? What if the people in the house refused to even believe that there was a problem? What if the very people that we were told to keep out could actually come in and help?

Not only did "what goes on in this house stays in the house" keep dysfunction in but it also prevented anyone sane from getting out. This mentality kept my family from getting help for the issues that lied just beneath the surface of our seemingly happy and healthy life. Even statistics show that if there is no intervention, children that come from homes where abuse or drugs are the norm are more likely to become addicted to drugs, become victims or perpetrators of violence, suffer from depression and anxiety and less likely to graduate from high

wow

school and enter the workforce. They are more likely to fail; fail in school and fail to complete school. More likely to fail to make good decisions, fail to raise their children, fail to deal properly with their emotions, fail to reach their goals in life and fail to be successful...Considering my genetics, DNA, family history and culture of not getting help, failure was much more likely for me than success. *wow*

What went on in our house did indeed stay in our house, get comfortable, eat, drink and grow until it was too big to hide anymore. I had barely scratched the surface one Sunday evening at Grandma Sugarlump's house.

Beneath the Surface

My dad had just fed us, given us a shower and my mother was ready to take us home. For some reason I was dressed but my younger brother Lou was not. My mother was ready to go and kept asking my father to place my little brother in her hands. My father argued that he wanted to get my brother dressed before giving him to my mother. Somehow the argument turned into a physical tussle and my mother grabbed my baby brother into her arms. I stood in the kitchen watching this argument as my mother and father continued to go back and forth at the top of the basement stairs. In what seemed like a matter of seconds, my mother and baby brother fell backwards down the entire flight of stairs and landed on the basement floor. Everything happened so fast I couldn't tell whether my father pushed them, backed them up or if my mother had just lost her balance and fell. My mother later confirmed what I didn't want to believe; my father had indeed pushed her. I was horrified and ran to the phone to call the police. At 4 years old I knew that 911 could be called to help in situations like this. What my 4-year-old little self didn't know was that 911 was a number and not a place. "What's the number to 911, I yelled, What's the number to 911, my mommy's hurt!"

Just beneath the surface of my family's beautiful covering lied the scars and bruises of Domestic Violence. Just like the "What goes on in this house stays in this house" mentality, it had been passed down through the generations. The women in my family had learned to throw some makeup on their bruises and keep it going. A punch, a black eye, a swollen face didn't stop no show, and certainly was not a reason to leave. Your face would heal, your bruises subside and your relationship with your abuser would go on as normal. I saw this scenario played out several times amongst my family members and eventually it became known as an expected part of a relationship. Domestic Violence made its debut in my life at 4 years old—and unfortunately stayed around for an encore several years later.

Little did I know that my family's refusal to address the secrets below the surface made it even more likely that I would struggle with these same problems at some point during my life. Coming into this world I was fighting against the very real possibility that I would become addicted to drugs, experience sexual abuse, become the victim in a physically abusive relationship, suffer from emotional disorders and earn very little income. The odds were stacked against me. How was I going to win and overcome these issues when from the very beginning I was set up to FAIL!

Surviving Against the Odds

Maybe you're like me and before you even had a say, some things in your life were chosen for you as a result of decisions your parents and grandparents made. Maybe the odds were stacked against you from birth. Maybe you were born to a single parent, the product of a rape, or given up for adoption. These are all decisions that you had no choice in. The world would want you to believe that because of these things you were born with a disadvantage. That you are doomed to failure and success is not likely. I encourage and challenge you not to believe the hype. The decisions your parents and ancestors made do impact you, but your story isn't set in stone. Maybe some of the chapters in your life were already written but guess who holds the pen now? You do, and your future is waiting to be inked! Here are some tips to help you rewrite your story.

Survival Tips

1. Refuse to be a Statistic

You can find any psychology book, scientific research or news report that will proudly proclaim that if you come from less than perfect circumstances you are somehow doomed to a life that's less than that of the average person. Focusing on and believing what the world says about you will cause you to fall into a self-fulfilling prophecy. A self-fulfilling prophecy is a phenomenon that states that when you believe negative things about yourself, you end up fulfilling or living out the negative things you believe. Instead of buying into and fulfilling the statistics, use the negativity as fuel to prove the world wrong. If your parents were drug addicts, statistics say you are likely to become an addict too. Make up your mind to stay away from drugs or anyone that may try to get you involved in drugs. Refuse to be the status quo and you will beat the odds.

2. Resist the Chameleon Syndrome

Chameleons are products of their environment. They go with the flow and change colors in order to fit in with their surroundings. A teenager living in the projects has no choice but to be surrounded by gang violence, poverty and drugs. They can choose to go with the flow and join their neighborhood gang or refuse to blend in and aim to connect with groups at school or positive groups in the community. Choose not to blend in and fit in the box of your circumstances. You can't change the cards you were dealt in life, but you can choose how you play your hands.

3. Be Better and Not Bitter

You may be angry about not knowing your dad or losing your mom. Or maybe you were born into a family who refused to give you love and attention. You have every right to be angry, upset and hurt, but you deserve to be happy and whole. Whatever your circumstances, choose to be better and not bitter. Choose to make better decisions than those before you and defy the odds with your resiliency instead of your resentment.

TWO

When Things Aren't What They Seem

Real Fake

As time went on my mother began to date. Most of her boyfriends I liked and never had a problem with. They never interfered with my relationship with my mother, and I still got to see my dad on weekends. As a single parent, my mother struggled, but my grandmother made sure we had everything we wanted and needed. My dad would cook for us and occasionally spend time with us when we were at his house. I actually enjoyed when my mom had a new male friend. In particular I liked Dean very much. He lived with us for awhile and he really was like a big kid.

Growing up in a household with 3 brothers, it should come as no surprise that I was a tomboy. Although I had my creative, artsy side, I looked up to my big brothers and wanted to do the things that they were interested in. I wore my hair braided to the back, baggy clothes, tennis shoes and I loved wrestling. When we had cable, we made sure to watch Monday night RAW and Thursday night SMACKDOWN. Dean was right there with us. Sometimes he would even let us order wrestling on Pay Per View. My brothers and I were so into wrestling that we all had wrestling names. I was Queen Bee, Lou was Killer Bee, Lee was Punisher and Lem was Lodi. We had wrestling matches in our house and Dean was often the referee. We got so into this wrestling thing that we took our federation to Grandma's house and invited our cousins to be a part of it. We had a women's league that consisted of myself, my cousin Tiosha (Apocalypse) and Minah (Memo).

My other cousins were involved too: Julius (Killer), Nando (Cybertech) and Monte. The wrestling soundtrack had come out around that time, so we all had music that we would walk out to. My grandmother had bought us wrestling belts and we competed against each other for the title. We would use the couches and stand on them as if they were the ropes during our entrance. We even had handicap matches where the boys would go against the girls—and of course we always lost. As kids, you tend to think that whatever you see on TV is real. We didn't know that the wrestlers were actually trained to do fake moves that seemed real just for the purpose of entertainment. We thought they really wanted to hurt each other for the sake of winning a title. So we imitated their behavior and sometimes allowed things to get a little too real. One of us would get hurt here and there, but a little blood never hurt anyone, right? Eventually we invited the whole street to be a part of our wrestling league and join our Royal Rumble matches in the backyard.

Outside of the wrestling ring, my mom was still my partner and my hero. Dean and my mom went their separate ways and although I missed him, I loved my mother very much and respected her decision. Little did I know that the world wrestling federation I loved and longed to be a part of wasn't the only thing in my life that really wasn't what it appeared to be.

Mr. Right

At first glance he seemed like a dream come true. Nelson was his name. He was very friendly, treated my mom well and he took my brothers and I to McDonalds. As an 8-year-old kid, whoever takes you to McDonalds instantly becomes your best friend. Most importantly though, he had a good and stable job. I was fully aware that my mother was a single parent of four and struggling to make ends meet even with my grandmother's help. Meeting someone who was willing to provide for 4 children that were not his own seemed like something out of a fairytale. He was definitely Mr. Right. After dating my mother for a while, Nelson moved in with us. He continued to live up to his heroic image until one Friday night.

For some reason, I was alone in the house with him while my mom took my brothers to visit my dad for the weekend. Nelson called to me from the living room in his heavy Hispanic accent, "Hey Courtney, come here for a second." I shouted back with enthusiasm, "Here I come." I liked having Nelson around. I didn't have any positive memories of my mother and father together so I thought it was pretty cool to have a dad in the house.

Nelson invited me into the living room and asked me to sit on the couch next to him. He put his arm around my shoulder and pulled me close to him. At first I thought this was his way of showing fatherly affection but then he began to caress me and hold me even closer. He draped his arm around my shoulder like we were a couple on a date at the movies. Like I belonged to him, like I was his and he was mine. As his sexual vibes increased, so did my anxiety. Nervous and all, I didn't want to jump to conclusions. I had never shared intimate father daughter moments with my dad so I didn't really know what they should feel like. I wondered what Nelson was doing but since I wasn't 100% sure I went with the flow.

Nelson leaned in and kissed me; working his way up my bare arms with his lips. In between kisses he asked if it felt good and if I was enjoying him. Even at 8 years old, I knew that although he did not undress me, his actions and intentions were sexual. I was afraid for what would come next so I asked to use the bathroom. He stopped kissing me and allowed me to excuse myself. I locked myself in the bathroom and began pacing the hard cold floor. "What in the world is he thinking?" I asked myself. Doesn't he know that I'm just a kid? I can't have sex with him. I don't even know how to have sex. How am I going to tell him no? Am I going to get in trouble? What if my mom finds out? Is she going to be mad at me? Questions that I didn't have the answers to seemed to cloud my brain. I knew that what Nelson had done was wrong but I didn't want him to get in trouble. I actually liked having him around and I didn't want to be the reason he left. I had a decision to make. I could either go back out there and give Nelson what he wanted or wait in the bathroom until my mother came home and risk Nelson being angry with me.

This decision was so stressful for me that I somehow blacked it out. The last thing I remember is trying to decide whether I was going to come out of the bathroom or not. To this day what happened next is foggy. I don't even remember how I ended up leaving the bathroom. I do know that after this day something in me changed. And something changed in Nelson also.

Jekyll and Hyde

The change in the relationship between Nelson and me became very evident. It went from a developing father/daughter relationship to hatred and disgust. I began to despise Nelson and no longer wanted him to be a part of our family. I didn't tell my mother about what happened that night but I began to feel that Nelson took all my mother's time and attention away from me. I often felt that my mother chose his side over mine. And then ever so slowly Nelson's true character began to show. He was really a wolf in sheep's clothing. A classic Jekyll and Hyde. He was nice and warm to my brothers and others yet developed an obvious disdain for me. We started arguing every day about the smallest things. I became the object of his anger and frustration. During this time Nelson became physically and verbally abusive towards my mother. I became aware of his abuse the night they got married.

A few weeks prior to the wedding, Nelson had decided that there had been so much tension between he and I that he wanted to "reconcile" and take me and my mother on a cruise. I was shocked at his idea seeing that we were constantly fighting like cats and dogs. We drove to Florida and took the Carnival Cruise to the Florida Keys and Mexico. We had a great time exploring the land and snorkeling. I had so much fun that I even considered forgiving Nelson. The last night on the cruise Nelson decided to propose to my mother in front of me and of course she said yes. I was livid. How in the world could she say yes to this man who obviously hated me and had approached me sexually (she was unaware of this at the time)? I had nothing to say to him or my mother. My mother mentioned that I should have said congratulations but in my mind there was nothing to celebrate.

When we got back to the U.S. my mother and Nelson went to the courthouse to get married. None of us children were invited to the wedding. In fact, we weren't even informed that they were getting married on that particular day. I was sitting on the couch when they stumbled through the door arguing and screaming. I immediately noticed the drops of blood on my mother's white dress and assumed that they had gotten into a fight. My mother yelled about how Nelson had put his hands on her while he screamed back about the scratches on his face. I could not for the life of me understand why my mother would endure this type of treatment all in the name of love. What kind of man would hit his wife on their wedding day? Nelson had never messed with my brothers. He didn't argue, yell or get physical with them. It was only with me and now with my mother.

Nelson's abuse continued and escalated. He started drinking heavily; several cans of beer a day. He took on more and more control by making plans to buy a house in his name and forbidding my mother to work outside the home. He took care of every one of our financial needs and wanted our total dependence to be on him. Nelson seemed to work overtime trying to tear apart the relationship between me and my mother, While driving in the car one day, Nelson and I started arguing. My mother asked me to be quiet more so out of fear of what he would do to her. He had developed this habit of punishing my mother when he was mad at me. Nelson took this opportunity to do just that. He drove to E.55th St and told my mother to get out of the car at the end of the freeway. He yelled at her to walk back to our home which was on W.88th in Denison. It was clearly the other side of town and separated by the freeway. Even if my mother found a way to walk through the streets, it would take her several hours to get home. Nelson kicked her out the car and drove away. He took me home as if nothing had ever happened.

Growing Apart

The wedge between my mother and me seemed to increase daily. It got to the point where I started writing in my journal and telling my mother that I was going to kill myself. Each time I wrote in my journal how I felt about Nelson, my mother and how horrible my life was, my mother would write little notes to me alongside my entries. She would write that she didn't hate me and that she loved me so much that she prayed to have a baby girl. I was the answer to her prayers. But her words didn't seem to line up with her actions. Once again, things weren't really what they seemed to be. My mother's words said she loved me, but her lack of action allowed her husband to treat me the way he did. I felt that my mother didn't take up for me, didn't defend me against Nelson and therefore loved him more than she loved me.

One day in the middle of a heated argument I told my mother that I was going to suffocate myself. I couldn't take living in the house with them anymore and the pain I was experiencing was too much. I had written a note to Nelson that detailed how much I hated him, that my suicide was going to be his fault and that my mother only stayed with him for his money. My mother argued with me and eventually wrestled the note away from me so that I would not give it to Nelson. I didn't attempt suicide that night but a deep rooted anger began to take its place in my heart.

Not only was I angry with my mother but I was disappointed and hurt that Nelson was not who he had appeared to be. I trusted him to treat me, my brothers and my mother well and he had failed to do that on so many levels. In my mind, the physical fights with my mother and daily arguments with me should have been enough for my mother to leave him. On top of the arguing, I knew that the incident on the couch was a sexual innuendo but had no proof and couldn't remember how far it actually went. Although my mom didn't know about that incident, I felt that what she did know about Nelson was grounds for ending the relationship. My anger toward him and my mother developed into an attitude of distrust and disdain. Eventually Nelson did discover that it was time to end the relationship—just not the relationship between him and my mother...

Surviving When Things Aren't What They Seem

When we're young, we're taught to trust adults—especially close family and friends. Unfortunately, the people closest to us are often the ones that can hurt us the deepest. They are usually seen as trustworthy by others and therefore given access to our hearts, minds and homes without our permission. This access can sometimes leave us vulnerable and as victims of molestation and betrayal. If you put your trust in someone and they turned out not to be who they appeared to be, know that you are NOT alone. If you trusted an adult to take care of you and they handled you inappropriately, I share your pain in this experience. You may have been victimized but survival is still possible.

Amir

Survival Tips

1. Release the Guilt

When something bad happens to us, we tend to look for someone to cast the blame on. As children, it is much easier to blame ourselves than to point the finger at a trusted adult. No matter who it was, what they said or how old you were, whatever happened to you was NOT your fault. The blame and responsibility lie solely on the adult that took advantage of you. Release the guilt by letting go of the blame.

2. Talk to Someone

If you are currently being molested or are a child that has been molested, I urge you to talk to someone. If you feel like you can't tell your parents, or if your parents are the ones who molested you, tell a teacher, guidance counselor, principal, youth leader or pastor. Tell an adult that you know will believe you and take action on what you share. If you are an adult that was molested as a child I encourage you to talk to someone as well. The wounds of the past can't heal if they are hidden or ignored. They must be uncovered and dealt with properly in order for healing to begin.

3. Remember that You are NOT what happened to you

These ugly unfortunate experiences do not dictate who you are or what you're worth. The mere fact that someone took advantage of you does not cancel out the fact that you deserve to be treated with loving kindness. Your experience may have left you feeling worthless, but you truly are worthy and good enough. You had no choice in becoming a Victim, but you can choose to be a Survivor.

THREE

In Second Place

Him vs Me

Over the next 2 years, Nelson and I argued so often that he told my mother something had to change. He was tired of going back and forth and in his mind there was only one way to solve this problem. Someone had to go, either him or me. I sat by the phone listening to the conversation my mother was having with my grandmother, telling her how they could no longer control me and that my behavior had gotten so severe. Nelson chimed in about how I was disrespectful and unappreciative of his involvement in my life. My heart dropped as my mother said, "We think it's best that Courtney stays with you." I couldn't believe it. I was 10 years old, being kicked out of my mother's house and sent to live with my dad and grandmother. Now don't get me wrong: When I was upset, I had often said I would rather live with my dad than put up with Nelson, but I never expected it to really happen. Nor did I expect Nelson to give my mother an ultimatum and tell her that if I did not move out, he was going to. I had never even been at my grandmother's house by myself; my brothers or cousins had always been there with me. My grandmother was elderly and my dad was a drug addict who was barely home. How were they going to take care of me?

I was already at my dad's house for the weekend so I was told to stay put and my belongings would be brought to me. My move out date was effective immediately and once again I had no say in the matter. I was forced to leave my brothers, friends, school and activities. Nelson made it clear that I was no longer welcomed in "his home" and could not return until he said so. In a matter of 2 years, the woman I had loved, admired and praised for being an amazing mom had now become the woman I hated and despised. The strength and independence she once exuded had now faded into weakness and dependence. Cie was no longer my mother but Nelson's wife and my enemy.

Me vs Them

Grandma Sugarlump, who was almost 70 at the time, welcomed me in her home. I had spent weekends and vacations there so it wasn't a completely unfamiliar place. My father and my sister Leena were also staying with my grandmother at the time. My dad had become what I call a functional addict meaning he could still function in everyday life (cook, clean, run errands) when he chose to even though he was addicted to drugs. I was fully aware of his habit but for some reason it didn't matter much to me. I was angry with my mom for kicking me out and choosing Nelson over me but I was never angry with my dad for choosing drugs over me. In fact I wanted to cling to him every chance I got. He never stayed in the house long and I knew that he could disappear at any moment. It took me just a few summers and weekend visits to learn his pattern. Usually after fixing Sunday dinner my dad would then ask if I wanted ice cream from the corner store. Of course I would say yes and he would head out the door, down the street, to the store. Even the slowest walker could make it there and back in 20 mins. That's including an extra 5 mins if you stopped along the way to talk to some friends. Somehow my dad would always get "lost" on his way to the store and not return for days.

When he finally did come back I would question him about his whereabouts and my ice cream. He took those moments as opportunities to leave again so he could go get the "ice cream" he had promised me. Each time he came back empty handed. Eventually I got hip to his corner store question and would tell him I didn't want anything from the store. I thought this would stop him from leaving but it didn't. So I upped my antics and started following him around the house to ensure that he didn't slip out the door. *new*

One particular day I was following him around when I noticed he had something in his hand that looked liked pills. "Hey dad, what's that?" I said, as I pointed to the little circle shaped pills in his hand. "Oh this?" he said as he quickly turned the palm of his hand up. "It's candy." I reached to grab it out of his hand but he was too quick for me. He closed his fist, drew back and said "You can't have this, this is adult candy!" Of course it is, I thought to myself. Adult candy called DRUGS! My dad knew that I was smart and wasn't buying his answer. He also knew that I was dead set against letting him slip out of the house again and not returning until God knows when. I continued to follow him around hoping this would prevent him from taking the drugs or at least keep him in the house even if he did take them. I walked behind him as he tried to find a place to escape to. Wherever he went I went. He walked to the door and I was right behind him. He stood at the window and I did too. Yes! Finally, I had him. He wouldn't dare take the pills right in front of me or walk out while I was watching. He wanted to keep his secret safe and I knew he wouldn't completely expose his addiction in front of me.

What I failed to realize was that my dad was an experienced addict and knew what to do to get me off his back even for just a few minutes. And a few minutes was all he needed to get his high. "I need to use the bathroom," he said. Crap! Now what was I going to do? I couldn't follow him in the bathroom but I didn't want him to leave or get high. So I walked with him to the bathroom and waited outside the door. I heard the toilet flush, the sink turn on and then he came out. "Good, I still got him," I thought. I turned to look at his hands and noticed that the "candy" was gone. Had he flushed them down the toilet? It only took a quick glance at his face to answer my question. Sweat beads poured from his forehead and he became extremely paranoid. No, he hadn't flushed them down the toilet. He had put them in his mouth and swallowed them.

I wasn't able to keep my dad from getting high but I was adamant about not letting him leave the house. Since I was only 10 and my dad was in his 40's, he always found a way to outsmart me. I was smart but he was smarter. The days I followed him around he would just wait until I fell asleep to slip out the door. Or he would pretend to go to sleep so that I would think he was in for the night. I'd close my eyes and if I woke up in the middle of the night to check on him, he would already be gone. Each time I woke up and saw that he was gone, it was a blow to my heart and a reality that I had failed again. I often wondered if one day he would just decide to never come back. Waking up became painful because I always hoped that I would open my eyes and still see my dad lying on the couch. And most of the times I didn't. After he had been gone for a few days he would return while I was sleeping. I never knew whether I was going to wake up and find him there or gone for an unknown amount of time.

While my dad was gone strange people would call and come to the house looking for him. I would search through his things in hopes of finding some clue to where he might be. Instead of finding clues I found needles and several IDs that belonged to other people. I often wondered if these were the strange people calling looking for their belongings. I worried about my dad's safety and if he would end up in jail or dead. Sometimes, while driving with my grandmother, I would see my dad out on the streets. I'd ask my grandmother to stop the car so I could get out and talk to him. I'd beg him to come home and he always promised he would but he wouldn't show up for days or weeks.

My brothers and cousins all knew that if my dad was home when they came over we had to take certain steps to keep our money and valuables safe. If we fell asleep with money on us, by morning it would be gone. It was nothing new that my dad stole from us. My grandmother knew this as well. If something came up missing grandma would replace it and encourage us not to make a fuss about it. The only way anyone's money would be safe around my dad was if it was placed on our bodies near a private part (in a bra or your underwear.) My dad never went under our clothes to search for money. Now if you left money laying out, in a purse, wallet, pockets, shoes, socks, you would never see it again. We had to hide anything valuable that could be sold for drugs. Even the pots and pans would come up missing! My whole family was fully aware that my dad stole from us to buy drugs, but no one ever addressed it.

Even though I knew all these things about my dad, nothing could stop me from loving him. I dreamed about being Daddy's Little Girl. All I wanted was to spend some time with him. I wanted him to love me just as much as I loved him. I wanted him to show me some affection and attention. Instead he gave his time, money and attention to drugs. He chose them over me and once again I was left in second place.

Me vs Me

Here I was, 10 years old, separated from my mother and looking for love from my father. I felt lonely, betrayed, angry and hurt beyond belief. I thought that no one loved me or understood me. How could my mother put Nelson first and allow him to send her only daughter away? What had happened to us? We had spent so much time together and now I couldn't even see her unless her abusive husband said so? How could she choose to live life with him and not me? How could my father choose to chase after a high instead of spending time with me? I had so many questions and my heart grew bitter.

My extended family was extremely upset with me. They were all disappointed in how I began to talk to and treat my mother and her husband. Everyone blamed me and could not understand why I would treat "such a good man" that way. They believed that because Nelson took care of a family of 6, including 4 children that were not his own, that he was a "good man." If they only knew that the material things he provided came nowhere close to making up for the abuse we suffered. *wow*

My time at my grandmother's was free of arguments and drama, but I spent most of my days alone. I changed schools and enrolled in Whitney Young Middle School. My grandmother frequently praised me for my academic success and my acceptance into a National Blue Ribbon School. Although I liked my new school and made friends quickly, I still missed being at home with my brothers. I wasn't used to being the only child in the house. After homework was done there wasn't much left for me to do. My sister was 19 and dating, my grandmother was elderly and my dad was in and out of the streets. No one spent a whole lot of time just hanging out with me like my brothers did at home. When my sister was home she did my hair, took me shopping, made sure I ate and occasionally allowed me to accompany her on dates. Other than our little excursions there wasn't much else to do. I tried out for and became a member of the Whitney Young Highsteppers team. I was glad about having something to do but I also felt like a traitor because Whitney Young was a long time rival of my previous school Wilbur Wright. *wow*

During this time, I decided to start going to church with my grandmother. Church was boring but I felt like going was the right thing to do. Even my grandmother thought it was boring. Every Sunday she would sit on the front row, pass out those church candies (butterscotch, peppermints, the strawberry candies), cough really loudly a few times and then go to sleep. Her routine never changed. I would often daydream about going back to my mother's house and what I had to do to make things right.

One day as the Pastor finished his sermon, he opened the doors of the church and called for those who wanted to be saved. I didn't quite know what he meant but my heart was pounding out of my chest so I figured it was my cue to go down. I went to the front of the church and I guess I got "saved." Shortly after, I was baptized and received a certificate of the events that took place that day. I didn't quite understand everything but I thought if my family knows that I got "saved," they will believe I've changed and my mom will convince Nelson to let me come back home. It was to my dismay when I discovered my "getting saved" tactic didn't work the way I planned. My family was happy for me but no one thought this gesture signified a change in behavior or that it was good enough to go home.

The angry, sad, isolated person I had become was not the Courtney I had once known. My family seemed to be falling apart and so was my identity. I had always thought I was a good person, fun and loving…I was an optimist who saw the glass half full. Now the glass seemed to be half empty and represented how I felt inside. My parents' decisions to prioritize what they loved most caused me to question everything I thought I knew. I began to believe that coming in first was no longer an option and second place was all I was worth.

Surviving in Second Place

We all want to win at some point in our lives, especially when it comes to being first in the lives of our loved ones. Coming in second can tend to make us feel rejected, not good enough or like we don't deserve to win. I need you to know that none of these things are true. Not being made a priority says less about you and more about the person choosing to overlook you. Second place is painful, but you can still make it to the finish line with your heart and mind intact.

Survival Tips

1. Believe that You Are Good Enough

We tend to develop our identity and thoughts about ourselves based on how others treat us. When we've been overlooked or rejected, we choose to believe it's because we're not good enough. This is NOT true. Someone calling a Diamond a Cubic Zirconium does not change the diamond's value or worth. It's still a Diamond regardless of if an individual considers it good enough to be one. YOU are Good Enough just because you were created. It has nothing to do with what you have or have not done. You're good enough just because.

2. Consider that You Were in the Wrong Hands

If a 6-year-old boy finds a Diamond, he's going to think it's a rock. He will kick it, throw it, step on it and play with it like a rock. But if a Jeweler finds that same Diamond, he'll recognize its potential, clean it up, put it through the fire and place it in a jewelry store where it's supposed to be. If you've been stepped on, played with and thrown around like a rock, please know that you were in the wrong hands. The individual you trusted may not have known how to care for you the way you deserved. Remember that you are a Diamond even if you've been treated like a Cubic Zirconium.

3. Forgive

Forgiveness is one of the most powerful tools that we were given to help heal our hearts and transform our minds. Forgiveness does NOT mean you are excusing the crime. It means that you are no longer willing to be the victim. Forgiveness is letting go of the power that the painful act has on your emotions and thoughts, whether the person deserves it or not. Even if they don't deserve your forgiveness you deserve freedom. Be free from your past by forgiving.

FOUR

As the Underdog

Friday Night Lights

After a year or so at my grandmother's, she passed away
and my mom and Nelson saw fit to bring me back home. This
arrangement worked out well—until my birthday. During my
grandmother's funeral I learned that I had a sister named Tilisha
on my father's side that I had never met. Upon meeting her I
wanted to hang out with her all the time. For my 12th birthday
I had planned to go skating with my cousin Minah and then
spend the weekend at Tilisha's house. I had worked really hard
on my behavior and stayed out of trouble with Nelson. He also
thought that my behavior had been pretty good so he and my
mom decided to take me shopping before dropping me off at the
skating rink.

The skating rink was my favorite place as a preteen. My

cousins (Aminah and Tiosha) and I would go skating at Zelma George Recreation Center every Friday. It was always packed with lots of teenagers and certainly the highlight of our week. You had to come dressed fresh from head to toe otherwise the kids would make fun of you. My shopping trip with my mom and Nelson was right on time! We walked into my favorite store, Lady Blue, and I scanned the wall for the perfect pair of shoes. My eyes fell on a pair of red and black high-top Air Force Ones. Nelson paid for the shoes and I could hardly contain myself. I couldn't wait to show them off. I slid them on at the register, laced them up and walked right out the store with the shoes on my feet! In the car I made sure my side ponytail was gelled up right, two swoops in the front and fanned out in the back. I just knew everyone was going to love my new look tonight. I did one last check before pulling up to the rink. Hair popped, check. Outfit fresh, check, shoes laced, check. It was my birthday, I was cute and ready to have some fun.

As we pulled up to Zelma George I saw Nelson's eyebrows raised in the mirror and he made a comment about how many boys were at the rink. I assured him that I wasn't coming for the boys but that I was interested in hanging out with my cousin and skating. I hopped out the car, waved goodbye and went into the rink. As I walked in, I could still see Nelson and my mom watching me from the window. Five minutes later they were still there. Nelson quickly motioned for me to come back out.

"Ugghh, seriously," I groaned. When I got back to the car Nelson said "hop in." I got back in the car thinking he wanted to have a conversation about boys and peer pressure but instead he drove off. *now*

"Wait a minute, why are we leaving?", I yelled. "There are too many boys here; you're just trying to be fast," Nelson said. "But, it's a public place; I can't control how many boys are here," I said fighting back tears. "You weren't even skating", he shot back. "But I just got here; you didn't even give me a chance! Plus, it was a backwards skate, and I was just waiting for them to call an all skate," I said. Silence filled the car. The tension was so thick you could cut it with a knife. "So wait, that's it, I can't go skating?" I screamed. Without batting an eye, Nelson said, "No!" I couldn't believe it. I had worked on my behavior, it was my birthday and now I couldn't go skating with my cousin because there were boys standing outside the rink! I was so frustrated. I took off my paper wristband and threw it towards the front of the car in Nelson's direction. This was not a good idea. He yelled, "Oh you want to throw something at me? Fine, I'm going to whoop your butt, just wait till I pull this car over."

Nelson and I continued to exchange a few choice words, and the argument quickly escalated. Seeing those boys outside triggered something in him and his anger shot through the roof. He pulled over in a parking lot, hopped out the car and headed towards the back seat for me. I knew that this was not going to be a regular whooping but it was going to be a fight and I was the underdog. My first thought was that my mother would protect me but I didn't want to count on her so I jumped out the back seat and took off running up Chagrin Blvd. I ran and ran until Nelson caught up with me and brought me back to the car. He grabbed me around my chest and slammed me on the concrete. He threw his hands around my neck and started choking me. I kicked him in the face and tried to scream for my mom's help. Nelson tightened his hands around my throat and lunged my head into the ground. I was determined not to go out without a fight. With every head bang into the ground, I returned the blows with a kick to the face or the gut. He tried his best to restrain me and somehow managed to get my socks and shoes off. He screamed at me and said, "You don't deserve to wear anything that I've bought you!" *wow*

I looked over and saw my mother still sitting in the car. She was screaming and crying but made no efforts to stop the fight. Nelson picked me up, put me back in the car and yelled at my mother to switch seats and drive. He told her to take me to my father's house. *wow*

Nelson sat in the passenger's seat and turned his body towards the back so he could keep an eye on me. He grabbed me by my neck again and this time tightened his grip. I tried to tell him I couldn't breathe, but his grip was so tight no words came out. I figured I only had a few minutes before he either choked me out or I ended up with some serious injuries. I had to find a way to get out of his grip to prevent either of those things from happening. I knew I couldn't overpower him and my mother wasn't going to help so I searched the back seat for something to hit him with. My eyes scanned the dark floor and I thought I saw what looked like a shoe. Yes! It was a shoe! I remembered that my cousin had accidentally left her shoes in the car and to my advantage these shoes had heels on them. I felt around in the dark until I clasped my hand around the bottom of the heel. I swung with all my strength and hit Nelson in the face with the heel. I swung again and again. Each time I hit him he would loosen his grip a little bit. I used those few seconds in between hits to try and yell out the window for help. No one seemed to notice or care. We rode like this for almost 20 minutes. If it wasn't for the gasps of air I was able to take in between the hits, I'm sure he would've choked me out.

Nelson yelled at my mother to drive faster and not to worry about me. My mother screamed and cried but not once did she tell him to stop or make any efforts to rescue me.

We pulled up at my dad's and Nelson loosened his grip. I jumped out of the car barefoot and ran towards the house. The gravel in the driveway felt like glass under my feet but I didn't care. I had one mission and one mission only: To get in the house and make Nelson pay. I ran into the kitchen and grabbed a butcher knife laying on the table. I felt like Nelson deserved to die and I was going to be the one to kill him, I turned with the knife in hand and headed towards the door. My aunt walked past the kitchen and saw me headed outside, crying with the knife in my hand. She grabbed me before I could get back to the car and said "What is your problem!?" In between tears and heavy sobs I managed to say, "I'M GOING TO KILL HIM!" She took the knife from me and demanded to know what happened. As Nelson and my mother walked up the driveway I pointed and said "He slammed me, hit my head on the ground, choked me and SHE," pointing in my mother's direction, "did nothing!!" My mother and Nelson started crying and asked to come in to tell their side of the story. I ran back in the house and flew up the stairs to tell my dad what happened. After telling about the night's events I begged my dad to beat Nelson up. My dad's response was, "Sweetie I don't want to go to jail tonight. I have warrants, and if I go downstairs I will kill him and then I'll have to go to jail."

I couldn't believe it. Where was my defender? Who would stand up for me and protect me? No one called the police or Children Services. My dad wouldn't even go downstairs to address the situation. When my other family members got wind of what happened, they all thought I was in the wrong. They took the standpoint that no matter what you should never disrespect your parents. They focused on the fact that I had cussed my mother out for not stopping the attack. No one seemed to pay any attention to the other facts which included Nelson slamming me (a 12-year-old girl) on the concrete, hitting my head on the ground multiple times, taking my socks and shoes and choking me all while my mother sat in the car screaming but never tried to stop him.

After many tears, choice words and trying to explain what happened, my mother and Nelson decided it was time for them to go home. They left me at my dad's house—barefoot, no socks, no shoes and one change of clothes at my sister's house across town.

Behind the Scenes

I stayed at my sister's house for some time and then was able to go back home. Whenever I would "act up" or get in trouble with Nelson I was always sent to a family member's house for a few days or a week to "learn my lesson." I was often sent to my grandmother (on my mom's side) and aunt's house as punishment for my behavior. I'm not sure what these visits at family's house were supposed to do but it didn't help one bit. It actually made me feel like no one in my family liked me except for my sister Tilisha. All of the other adults expressed their disapproval in my actions towards my mother and Nelson. I felt alone and as if no one understood or even cared to ask why I was misbehaving.

No one seemed to notice that out of my mother's 4 children Nelson only bothered me. He did not mess with my brothers at all. He didn't yell, scream or argue with them; only me. It was later suggested to me in counseling that Nelson may have been angry with himself for being sexually attracted to me or ashamed about how he had approached me. His sexual attraction to me would also explain why he got so angry at the skating rink about the boys being outside. Which was extremely irrational, seeing that I had no control over who stands outside or the ratio of boys to girls in a public setting. My mother was among those who never questioned why Nelson only had a problem with me.

As time went on Nelson thought it was best to give my brothers and me our own living quarters. He bought us a two family house and he and my mother moved downstairs while my brothers and I lived upstairs. They came upstairs to cook and make sure we were ok but that was about it. The interesting thing was that during this entire time we seemed to function like a "normal family." My brothers and I participated in sports, activities and always had friends over. I played basketball, danced in high stepping, modeled and participated in beauty pageants. I won the title of Miss Cleveland Teen, Young Miss New York East Coast USA and participated in several modeling competitions. My mother and Nelson attended every game, competition and event. We had all the best shoes, clothes and what seemed like a wonderful family.

We covered up so well that no one would've ever guessed what was really going on behind the scenes. Our façade had fooled everyone and we seemed like the model family. In the eyes of others Nelson won "The Heroic Step Dad Award" and my mother appeared to have chosen "Mr. Right." She didn't have to work and Nelson paid for anything and everything her children wanted to do. A single mom's dream come true. When the spotlight turned off and the cameras went away, our dream life was really nothing more than a dream—a smokescreen, certainly not a reality. If one was given a backstage pass, they'd see that our lives were staged. Behind the scenes lied fear, anger and abuse towards my mother and me.

Academic Champ

Although my behavior at home was problematic, academically I shined. My mother took notice that my love for learning followed me throughout the years and that I seemed far more advanced than my peers. Learning came easy for me. I loved to read, write, draw, paint and dance. I had it honest. My creative ability came from my mother, and she allowed me to participate in activities that drew that creative side out. I was passionate about learning, but I was pretty embarrassed about being smart. Starting school early at 4 years old meant I was always a year younger than my classmates. Not only was I a year younger, but also I was always in the Gifted and Talented or Advanced classes. Being younger than everyone was bad enough, but taking classes that were two grades ahead of the actual grade I was supposed to be in was the icing on the cake. I told very few people my real age because I was afraid of being called a baby or a nerd. Being smart wasn't cool yet, and I certainly didn't want to be considered "lame."

As my last year of middle school came to a close, my mother insisted that I apply to an advanced school instead of going to the public school down the street. It was a new school called Early College, designed specifically for advanced students who wanted to accelerate their high school career. The program allowed students to complete a year's work in 3 quarters instead of 4 and then advance to the next grade. When students reached their 3rd year in the program, they were given the opportunity to take college classes for free at Cleveland State University along with their high school classes. Early College required a 3.7 GPA for admission and in spite of all the mess that was going on at home I had a 3.8 GPA. Even with Nelson's craziness, going back and forth between my mother's and father's house, missing school when I went to stay with family members, and all of the arguments and incidents, my grades never suffered. I loved school; it was my getaway. I really didn't want to go to another school with all smart kids because even amongst them I would still be the youngest. I was looking forward to going to the school where my brothers and all my friends went. I was honestly thinking more about socializing than having a good future. My mother continued to insist that I at least give Early College a try. With much resistance I applied, was accepted and went to an all honors high school at age 13.

My academic future was bright. My fight with life to this

point had resulted in a number of losses and bruises. But when I was in the ring with school, I always won. Learning was easy and I secretly enjoyed being smart. This was one fight that I was determined not to lose. I committed with all my heart, mind and soul to becoming the Academic Champ.

Surviving as the Underdog

What's that saying? You win some, you lose some. Fighting has been a part of the human reality as long as we've existed on this earth. We fight to live, fight to die, fight to overcome, fight to win but no one wants to fight to lose. It would defeat the whole purpose of fighting. The hard facts are that there are some fights in life you'll come out a champ and others you won't. There are certain battles in life that we all have to fight and then there are some that should have been fought for us.

The Underdog is a competitor that's thought to have little chance of winning a fight or contest. If you're like me and you've been fighting all your life as the Underdog, I identify with your scars and bruises. I know you may be tired and feel like throwing in the towel, but you can't give up now. You were built to survive.

Survival Tips

1. Get Help

There's strength in numbers. Whatever you're fighting in life, know that you don't have to do it alone. If you're a teen and your fight is physical, tell your teacher, guidance counselor or a parent. If your fight is against a parent, contact your local Department of Children & Family Services or call 911. If you're an adult and your fight is physical, call the police, a local domestic violence shelter or the National Domestic Violence Hotline at 1-800-799-7233. Whether your fight is physical, emotional or professional there are resources out there to help you. Someone, somewhere, has been in your position and survived. Type your need in a search box on the internet and you'll be surprised what comes up.

2. Share your Story

There is amazing healing power that comes when you share your story. It has double benefits. Sharing what you are or have experienced gives you an opportunity to get things off your chest. It also releases little chemicals in your brain called endorphins that make you feel better. The second benefit is that sharing your story can encourage others. They may be going through the exact same thing you've experienced. And it sure does feel good to know that you aren't the only one in the fight.)

3. Tap into your Resiliency

The definition of resilient means able to withstand and spring back into shape after being bent, stretched or compressed. We all have the ability to overcome difficult life situations—even those that may have crushed us or left us broken. Tap into your inner voice that says "I can do this." Choose to believe that what didn't kill you made you stronger.

From Victim to Survivor

FIVE

When it's Time to Go

Leaving

During my freshman year of high school my mom miraculously decided that she had had enough of Nelson's abuse and it was time to go. After a few years of waiting around for things to change, my mother had given up hope in the possibility of a good life with Nelson. Nothing had gotten better. He continued to drink heavily, control my mother's every move, argue with me and physically abuse her. I don't know which straw broke the camel's back, but I sure was glad that we were going far away from Nelson. My mother shared the news one evening at a secret family meeting. Before Nelson had come along, we would have monthly family meetings. During these family meetings we would talk about chores, who was responsible for what and our dinner menu for the month. Once Nelson was involved, family meetings were not as frequent, so we knew something was up.

My mom came upstairs to our area and instructed us to close all the vents. Nelson was downstairs and she wanted to make sure nothing she said traveled through the vents and got back to him. She gathered us in the living room and told us to have a seat. She took a deep breath and whispered, "We're leaving." I couldn't believe it! Those words were music to my ears. If Nelson wasn't just a floor below us I would've screamed, jumped and ran around the house. I had waited so long to hear those words. But then I remembered something: Nelson was not the type that was just going to let us leave, which is why he was unaware of our meeting. My mother stressed that us leaving had to be a secret. We could NOT tell Nelson for any reason. How was a family of 5 with no money (Nelson had all the money) going to leave without this man noticing? I listened more intently for her plan.

I knew that my mom knew how to survive at all costs. She had been a victim of incest, rape, domestic violence and poverty very early on in life. The situation with Nelson was not her first rodeo. Although emotionally and mentally she had been on autopilot for a while, it seemed as though her natural survival instincts kicked in and now leaving was about protecting her children. So what was her plan?

My mother told us she was going to get a job or two, work and save so we could have enough money to get a place of our own. My mother knew that this wouldn't be easy because Nelson didn't allow her to work. She had all the skills and experience to work but financially Nelson made enough to take care of all of us so she didn't have to work. Not working was also his way of keeping tabs on my mother. The only time she was allowed to work was with him. He had started his own construction company on the side and would make my mother work on construction projects with him. My mother was the artsy, free spirited type; building concrete walls was not something she was interested in. But he gave her no other options.

Taking everything into consideration like a good Survivor does. My mother knew that she had to have a Plan B. Just in case she wasn't able to work or get enough money, my mother came up with a backup plan for getting out of there. We discussed splitting up and going to different family members' houses to live. My mother didn't want to put a burden on anyone by bringing in a family of 5, so we talked about sending my brothers to one place, me going somewhere else and my mom going to the homeless shelter. Although I was ready to get away from Nelson, I couldn't bear the thought of my mother having to live in a shelter. I thought to myself, if push came to shove, maybe we could both go stay with my aunt and grandmother.

As my mother talked, I started daydreaming about who I would go on to live with. I wanted to go live with a friend of mine or get adopted by some rich family. If those weren't options, then I would beg my mom to come with me to my aunt and grandmother's house. My thoughts of being somewhere safe and happy were interrupted by sudden feelings of fear and anxiety. We had talked about places to go but one questioned still remained...How were we going to get there? The car belonged to Nelson and even if we took the car how were we going to fit all of our furniture and stuff in there? How were we even going to make it out the house without Nelson noticing?

My mother told us to start putting our items in boxes and throw clothes over the boxes so that Nelson couldn't tell we were packing and she would take care of the rest. She didn't know how we were going to get our things out of the house without alerting him, but she knew that somehow, some way, we were getting out of there.

The Escape

My mother started working somewhere and would stay gone during the day. I remember overhearing a conversation about how Nelson had found out where she was and began to harass her at her job. He harassed her so much that she lost the job. My mother was determined to get us out of there so she found other ways to make money. She went to the blood banks as often as she could to donate blood and plasma for a few dollars. Weeks of poking and prodding turned her light brown arms black and blue. The size and color of her bruises were enough to _wuv_

make anyone cry. My mother picked up some shifts somewhere doing clerical working and running errands for others here and there. Her goal was to do whatever she could to make ends meet and get us away from Nelson. _wcw_

It wasn't long before Nelson started to take notice of my mother's frequent absence. One day after school he came upstairs and asked where my mother was. We all told him that we didn't know and hadn't talked to her. Nelson let it go at first but then his questions quickly became a part of our daily routine. It was obvious that he didn't believe us and it was only a matter of time before he would begin to retaliate. He came up to our area to ask his daily questions about my mother's whereabouts but this time he had a plan. He waited until we answered all his questions the same way we normally would and then responded, "Ok, fine then." He went back downstairs and slammed the door. Whooh, we had made it through another one of Nelson's Q and A's. Our heavy sighs of relief were quickly interrupted by darkness. The lights went out and the heat stopped blowing. We sent Lance down to tell Nelson what happened and he came back with a report that shocked us all. Nelson was fully aware that the lights and heat were off, in fact he had shut them off and was refusing to turn them back on until he got some answers. We couldn't believe it. He was going to make us sit in the dark with no heat until we either (A) Told him where my mother was or (B) Until my mother got home. Nelson wanted answers that we were not willing to give him. So we sat in a cold, dark house.

Nelson knew that this move would force my mother's hand. She either had to choose between working and knowing her children would be at home in the cold and dark, or staying home but not being able to earn the money to move. With the way things were going I figured there was no way we would get enough money to move into a place of our own. Maybe Nelson had us trapped after all. Just when I thought we'd never be able to leave my mother called us in for another secret meeting. She informed us that she had emptied out the college funds my grandmother had set up for my 2 older brothers. She apologized to them and explained that we needed to use this money to move. See, Nelson was smart but my mother was smarter. She had worked out a deal with our former landlord who was my childhood best friend's father. My mother explained to him that we were trying to flee an abusive situation and in need of a place to stay. He agreed to let us move back in for little money.

We had already been packing all along and now we had the money to leave and a place to go. But how were we going to get out? My mother told us she had rented a U-Haul truck for the next day and we were going to move while Nelson was at work. She told us we had to move fast because he only worked an 8-hour shift and we had to be gone before he got back. This meant we only had time and space for our personal belongings and stuff in our bedroom. Most of our furniture had to stay. The next day, when Nelson went to work we loaded our items into the truck and pulled off. We escaped without notice in less than 7 hours. wow

Settled In

When we got back to our old house I was terrified that Nelson was going to find us and make us come back. I thought if he knew where we lived, he would harass us until we had no choice but to give in to his demands. One day as my brothers and I were walking to the grocery store, an orange two door truck pulled up alongside of us. The driver yelled, "Hey Guys!" Immediately we recognized the voice. It was Nelson. My stomach tied itself in little knots, my heart pounded out of my chest and worked its way up my throat. I thought to myself, "There's no way he could kidnap all four of us right?" I wondered if he'd follow us until we led him to our house or maybe force us to give him our address. Surprisingly he did none of the above. He said a few words then drove off. We were certain at that point that he knew where we lived but for some reason he stayed away.

We settled into our home with our bedroom furniture, clothes, shoes and not much else. We had no money, couches, tv, car, washing machine or dryer but we were safe. And our safety was what mattered the most. Finally, the 5 of us were back together again. No abuse, no arguments, no separation and most importantly NO NELSON! I realized I wasn't the same little 8-year-old girl that I was the last time we lived in this house. Things had drastically changed over the last few years, and I hoped that they would get better. I looked forward to a new beginning and restoring the relationship with my mother. I had missed our talks, mother/daughter outings and dancing together. Now that Nelson was out of the way, we could pick back up where we left off. I just knew that once we got settled in my mother would sit me down and explain how sorry she was for everything that had happened to me. I waited eagerly for our conversation.

I waited for mother to apologize for the abuse I witnessed and endured. I waited for her to say sorry for all the nights that I laid in bed listening to her and Nelson argue. I waited for her to apologize for her blood-stained wedding dress. I waited for her to give an apology for his drunken stupors. I waited for her to say I'm sorry for not protecting you when Nelson attacked you. I'm sorry for separating you from your brothers and sending you to your elderly grandmother and drug-addicted father. I'm sorry that you had to sit in the dark with no heat until I came home. I'm sorry that I never asked you what you were thinking or feeling. I'm sorry that you had to pack up your things in fear and worry about Nelson coming after us. More importantly, I waited for her to say a few words that would have been the remedy for all. Words that would've soothed my soul and made everything alright. "I'm sorry for choosing Nelson over you; it'll never happen again." I waited for days to hear these words. Days turned into weeks and weeks turned into months. These words never came. No apologies ever came. We just kept on going with life as if nothing had ever happened.

Surviving When it's Time to Go

Leaving a loved one, a place or a connection is never easy. Even if the connection is unhealthy, separating can be painful. We are creatures of habit and tend to stay where we feel comfortable. You may know someone who is being mistreated but refuses to break ties. You may wonder why they don't just get up and leave if things are really that bad, but leaving is easier said than done. If your emotional, mental or physical safety is at risk, it's time to go. The process may be painful, but the temporary pain you will experience if you leave doesn't compare to the long term damage that would be done if you stay.

Survival Tips

1. Safety First

If you are leaving an abusive partner you'll want to consider your safety and the safety of any children involved first. Be sure to look at Survival Tip #2 (Have a Plan) which is necessary in keeping you and your children safe. In all other situations consider this: Is your emotional and mental health at risk? Are you torn down with words, ridiculed, embarrassed, made fun of, threatened or manipulated? Are you not allowed to have friends or isolated from family members? If so, your safety may be at risk, and it may be time to go.

2. Have a Plan

This tip is crucial if you're leaving a physically abusive partner. Think 2, 3 steps ahead and consider all your options for help. Contact family, friends or a domestic violence center so that you can have a place to go. If you are able to, save up some money so you're not restricted by finances. Once you leave, only disclose your whereabouts to those you can trust not to share with your partner

3. Find an Accountability Partner

When leaving a physically, emotionally or mentally abusive relationship, it helps to have someone keep you accountable. Most women leave and return to an abusive situation 7 times before they leave for good. When you have someone you can trust to remind you of your commitment to leave and help you along the way, it lightens the load a little bit. ⌒✓

From Victim to Survivor

SIX

On Purpose

Longing for More

As I mentioned before, my mother had gone into autopilot mode—like the lights were on but no one was home. The experience with Nelson was just as, if not more, traumatic for her than it was for me. My mother had already been the victim of incest, gang rape, domestic violence and her life had been threatened on several occasions. The years of craziness with Nelson only added to her list of unresolved trauma. It was easier for her to keep going and at least try to function than to stop and take time to address years of abuse. We were away from the most recent abuser and what mattered most was that we had a roof over our heads, food to eat and clothes on our backs. Anything else, emotions included, were secondary or not mentioned at all.

As a result of this, repairing the relationship between my

mother and me was not a top priority. It was as if leaving our old house was also supposed to mean leaving behind any thoughts, emotions or discussions about what we had experienced. My mother never asked me how I felt or what I was thinking. I had a lot of friends at school. I was smart and attractive, so on the surface I seemed to be doing well. Emotionally, however, I was a wreck. I didn't feel loved or affirmed by either of my parents. I felt indescribable voids and often thought I was crazy. I figured there had to be something wrong with me in order for my parents not to love me the way I deserved. My mother didn't protect me, and every time I looked up my father was always leaving me. They both had something that they loved more and put first in their lives. My mother, Nelson; my father, drugs.

I too began to long for more and wanted to be loved by someone—anyone. I knew that finding "love" wouldn't take me long, and I began my search among men. I talked to whoever would pay me some attention and acted like they liked me. One thing my mother had taught me was to survive at all costs, to find a way to get your needs met no matter what you had to go through. I had learned that whatever decisions you made and whatever people you connected with needed to be beneficial in helping you keep your head above water. People were resources and could help you get what you wanted out of life. My mother never directly said this, but this was the message I had picked up based on her relationship with Nelson. At 14 I was now able to reflect back on my mother's relationship. I realized that she didn't stay with him because she loved him, she stayed with him to survive. She stayed with him because financially her children didn't want for anything with Nelson in the picture. She stayed with him because he provided a roof over our heads, clothes on our backs and he funded every activity we wanted to participate in. My mother assumed that these things made us happy and that she could not provide for us on her own. In this way, it made sense to keep Nelson around as long as possible. new

Street Smarts

My mother was now responsible for taking care of a family of 5 on her own. My grandmother was gone, and my father didn't pay child support. My mother wasn't able to get the kind of job she deserved due to falsely being accused of a crime. We had food stamps, but they didn't always carry us through the month. During those times my mother would go down to the Salvation Army or other food pantries to make sure we ate. When my mother came home with a box full of off-brand random food items like meat in a tube or a block of cheese, I knew things were really bad. We didn't have a washing machine, and the laundromat was several streets away. So we did laundry all on the same day about once a month. In the meantime, if we needed something washed before laundry day, we had to improvise. We'd put our clothes in the sink, fill it up with water and detergent, grab a toothbrush to scrub out any stains, wring the clothes out and then put them up on hangers to dry. Occasionally, we'd come home and the lights or hot water were off. My mom always made sure she apologized and then found a way to put something on the bill to get the utilities back on. I hated going without and to see my family struggle so I knew I had to do something to get our needs met. I remembered that people were resources and connecting with the right people could change things. My survival instincts kicked in and I made it a point to get what I needed.

My time at Early College was cut short due to conflict with other students. I transferred to the public high school and made my debut in the middle of the year. Transitioning was easy because I had either gone to elementary or middle school with most of the students. Both of my older brothers were already there and popular, so it made my entry a piece of cake. My new school was in the inner city of Cleveland where most of the 1500 students came from low-income households. On any given day you could expect to see police officers walking around the school, metal detectors, fights and drug busts, but it was normal to us. In fact, I seemed to catch the attention of most of the drug dealers. And like a bee to honey, I was drawn in.

I was lured in by the fancy clothes, cash and custom cars. Finally, I could get what I needed: money and love. I was the new girl and the talk of the school (although probably not in a good way) because I had connected with almost all of the drug dealers in the area—and there were a lot of them! These guys were my bread and butter, and they all served a different purpose. There were some that I actually liked and others that got me the things I wanted and needed. When it was cold outside and I needed a ride to school, I had a "friend" I could call to pick me up. When I needed some new clothes or shoes, I had another friend I could call. When I needed to get my hair done or pay for things like school dances, I had another friend I could call. When I wanted to go to dinner or get my nails done, I had another friend I could call. When we didn't have any food in the house, I had a friend who'd drop off a pizza. And when I wanted some love and attention, I had a plethora of friends to choose from. Whatever the case, I always had a friend who could help out.

I bet you're wondering how I got all these "friends" and what I gave them in exchange for their gifts. The first thing that probably comes to mind is sex or sexual favors…but actually I didn't use my body. I used my purpose.

Purpose Discovered

Each guy served a different function in my life but I had one thing in common with all of them. I wanted to help solve their problems. The way my life was set up I had no choice but to be a problem solver. Remember, I was set up to fail. I was fighting against the odds and I was determined not to lose. Winning meant continuously finding solutions to life's problems.

I enjoyed problem solving, and I did it well. I knew that whatever I ended up doing in life, it was going to revolve around helping others. I dreamed of one day becoming a psychologist but in the meantime I was satisfied being the girl everyone talked to about their problems. It made me feel good to know that I could help someone feel better about different things they were facing. It made me feel like I had a purpose—a reason to keep fighting.

I'm sure the guys' interest in me was sparked by physical attraction at first. But then they were drawn in emotionally through listening and encouragement. I had a strange ability to see potential in others where most didn't. Even though drug money is what paid for my needs and wants I wasn't in favor of the drug culture. I didn't smoke or drink and didn't tolerate it around me. I knew what drugs had done to my dad and I hated that other families were being destroyed. So I won their respect by listening to their problems and encouraging them to do better. I often asked how they got into selling drugs and would encourage them to quit while they were ahead. Since most of them were in the streets to take care of their families, I'd tell them to get a legit factory job that paid decent money. I'd point out that the same skills needed in the streets (math, investing, flipping) could be used in a real profession like real estate, accounting, investing and corporate positions.

Many of them told me they had never even had anyone ask them about their thoughts and feelings. No one had taken the time to ask them about their future or what kind of life they wanted to live in 10 years. The streets were about getting immediate gratification and making sure everyone ate. That had been their only focus.

So I gained their respect, love, loyalty and money by using my natural abilities. I learned to kill 2 birds, love and money, with 1 stone: Purpose.

Surviving on Purpose

Oftentimes our purpose is found in our natural abilities. No one ever taught me how to help others solve their problems; it was just innate, something I was able to do with little effort. Now I'm by no means condoning involvement or connecting with others involved in illegal activity, or suggesting that anyone do as I did. This part of the story is for conceptual purposes only. The goal is to imitate the concept and not necessarily the specific behavior. The concept is that you can survive on purpose! I survived this period of my life financially and emotionally because I discovered and acted on my purpose. You may feel like you are wandering aimlessly or have nothing to live for, but please know that you were created with a goal in mind! And that goal has something to do with the greater good of others. Here's how you can survive on purpose.

Survival Tips

1. Discover your Purpose

What are you able to do that's been a natural gift for years? What gets you excited and stirs up passion when you talk about it? What would you be doing if you didn't have your current obligations like work, school, etc.? Asking yourself these questions can help you discover what your purpose is in life. That thing that gets you all riled up is usually a clue to what you can do to help others.

2. Share your Dreams

Tell someone you trust what you're passionate about doing, even if it hasn't been done yet. Accept only POSITIVE Constructive Feedback. Ignore anything from Negative Naysayers. Having someone affirm and believe in your purpose gives you that extra push to survive against the odds. Don't have someone to share with? Find a life coach in your area or one that offers sessions via webcam or phone. Many coaches offer free initial sessions that will empower you to get on track.

3. Connect

The internet and social media can be powerful tools if used correctly. Look for people who are doing or want to do what you feel you are called to do. Inspiration from like-minded individuals can make you feel like you have a mission in life. Discovering your reason to survive can save not only your life but also the lives of others.

From Victim to Survivor

SEVEN

A Change in Direction

Turning Point

One day, I came home from school and my mother told me that my cousin Ronald Watson had offered me a job. I was still only 14 at the time and didn't know much about Cousin Ron. I knew that he owned his own business, worked in a fancy office downtown and his wife, Cousin Anita, was my doctor. I thought to myself, "Why does he want me to work for him?" My two older brothers were already working, and Cousin Ron knew I was next in line to enter the workforce. I later found out that Cousin Ron saw all the potential in me that he saw in my mother. The potential to be great and excel in life. He also saw the potential to get caught up and make some bad decisions. He had watched as my mother gave up on her college career at a top school to be with my father. He knew about the abuse my mother had suffered and her struggle to take care of us financially. Cousin Ron didn't want history to repeat itself, so he thought it best to take me under his wings. That afternoon I caught the city bus downtown with much anticipation and excitement. I had been to Cousin Ron's office before, but only with my mom and my brothers, never by myself. I didn't quite know what to expect; I was just excited to make some money!

I pressed the button and rode the elevator up to the fourth floor. I stepped out and walked confidently down the hall. "Look at me, I'm a business woman!" I thought to myself. I knocked on the door and Cousin Ron met me with a friendly smile. "Hey lil Cuz," he said. "Let me show you to your office!" My office!? What in the world was going on, and why was he being so nice? I waited for the catch, but there was none. Cousin Ron wanted me to come in every day after school for 2 hours to do some secretarial work and then agreed to give me an actual check. I couldn't believe it. He taught me how to file, make copies, type, keep track of the company expenses, and write and deposit checks.

As soon as I started making a little money, my brothers told me they were no longer responsible for me so I had to start buying my own things. I had to pay for my cell phone bill and any other items I wanted. By the time we had moved away from Nelson, Lee and Lem were working jobs after school and in the summer. Lee was responsible for buying Lou's clothes, shoes, etc., and Lem was responsible for taking care of me. When they got new things, Lou and I did as well. My mom put her money toward paying the bills. Although I had to completely buy my own things now, I loved having a job and being productive. Things seemed to be turning around for me.

Where are We?

The summer came, and I was introduced to Cousin Ron's younger sister, Provi. Provi was light-skinned, slim, mixed and had a beautiful smile. Everyone thought we were twins or at least sisters. We hit it off right away and she invited me over to stay the night at Cousin Anita and Cousin Ron's house. Cousin Ron came to get me in his beige Jaguar, and we made our way to the suburbs. I felt like a famous celebrity being chauffeured to my next event. As we turned the corner to their street, I thought my eyes were playing tricks on me. Every lawn was lush green, manicured and landscaped. People walked down the street with their cute little dogs and waved with their leash in hand. I had never seen anything like it. How was it possible to have such a nice house in such a nice neighborhood? Where were we anyway? We pulled into the driveway, and with the click of a button, Cousin Ron opened the garage. I walked in and was greeted by Cousin Anita and two little dogs.

Their house was huge! It boasted high ceilings and white

carpet. It seemed like they had two of everything. Two living rooms (a den and formal living room), two tables (one in the dining room and one in the sun room) and two sets of couches. We didn't even have 1 couch and here they had 2 full sets! The first floor also housed an office, half bath and entry to the finished basement. Upstairs consisted of 4 bedrooms and 2 bathrooms. To me, it was a mansion. I made up my mind right then and there that I was going to be like Cousin Anita and Cousin Ron. And I was willing to do whatever it took to get there!

Provi and I had so much fun that eventually she invited me to stay the summer there and my cousins were glad to have me. I loved being at their house, but they had one particular rule I wasn't accustomed to: Everyone had to go to church. Now, I wasn't afraid to go to church, but I wasn't a big fan either. My only experiences with church had been at my grandmother's church as a little kid. Back then, going to church with her was an option. Now it was a rule.

The New Kids on the Block

The church they attended was hosting their Vacation Bible school for youth, and of course Provi and I were required to go. It was there that I met a lady who would help change the rest of my life, Rhonda Harrell. She was the youth pastor at the time and, along with Roy and Gail Matthews, she led the workshop sessions for my age.

Provi and I were wrapped up in conflict as soon as we

began to mix with the other kids in our vacation bible school class. We were the new kids on the block, we weren't "saved," we didn't belong to the church AND we got the attention of the boys. This was enough to make the girls who had grown up together gang up against us. A few times the Matthews had to stop class and address the arguing between each girl group. One particular day, an argument started outside during lunch. Seeing that we were already outside, it seemed like the perfect place to fight. The young lady and I got into each other's faces, talking and pointing at one another but before any blows could be thrown Pastor Rhonda called everyone back inside. She had no idea what was going on but she could definitely sense the tension in the room. She told all of us to go find a corner and ask God for forgiveness for whatever had happened.

I had no idea why I needed to ask for forgiveness since these girls had ganged up on me and Provi from Day 1, but I respected Pastor Rhonda, so I did what she asked. I kneeled down in the corner and folded my arms across my chest. My 5-second attitude was interrupted by a soft, beautiful voice. Pastor Rhonda had begun singing ever so sweetly and gently. In moments I found myself amongst the other kids crying and feeling sorry about the argument I had with the young lady. We ended up hugging and apologizing to each other. I asked myself: Who was this Pastor Rhonda, and how was she able to help me forgive just by singing?

During this group I began to think more about God. I started asking a million and one questions and pondering the answers Pastor Rhonda was giving. At the end of the vacation bible school, Pastor Rhonda invited all of us to take a pledge not to be sexually active and save ourselves until marriage. I was scared to take that pledge because I was afraid that God would kill me if I couldn't keep it. I didn't want to commit to anything I wasn't ready for yet, but I treasured this idea in my heart. Another young lady, Delores Rose, invited me to the church for youth Sunday. I had started working at McDonalds on the weekends but I figured missing a Sunday of work to go to church was a good reason. I requested off and attended my first youth service.

Come About

I walked into the church and felt such love and warmth. As the service went on, the people began to lift their hands and dance. I laughed to myself and thought these people are crazy, but I sure am enjoying this. And then Pastor Rhonda took the pulpit to preach for the last time for several years. I don't even know what she was preaching about, but I was captivated and felt like I could actually relate to her. She seemed real, passionate and genuinely interested in making a difference in the lives of young people. And I admired her for that.

As time passed, I took another Sunday off to attend church. This time I sat with Cousin Anita way in the back. The choir began to sing and I found myself standing up. I didn't know the song they were singing but suddenly I felt like something was missing. I started to think about this emptiness and my longing to be loved and affirmed. My hands slipped up and before I knew it tears were streaming down my face. Here I go again crying because of singing! As the choir sung I thought about the abuse I had experienced; the relationship with my mother; the nonexistent relationship with my father; the fact that I felt unloved, not good enough, broken and damaged. I cried because for the first time, I realized how angry and hurt I was that my life had not gone the way I expected. I cried because the love, warmth and acceptance I felt sitting in this church was something I had never experienced before. And in that moment I felt a glimpse of hope. Maybe my life would get better, maybe I wouldn't suffer forever, maybe I could be loved, emotionally whole and complete.

My thoughts were interrupted by Cousin Anita gently grabbing my hand and leading me to the front of the church for prayer. This time I welcomed the idea of being "saved" with no other motive than to feel complete and have an encounter with God. My days of trying to earn brownie points with my family were over. I wanted to know who God was, and if he really loved me or not. The prayer was beautiful, sweet, peaceful, and amazingly overwhelming. These people didn't know me. They didn't know how bad I was, what I had experienced, the horrible things that I had said to my mother. Yet they prayed for me as if I were their own, as if I were someone who deserved forgiveness and love. I was so overwhelmed with joy and relief that I could not stop crying. I cried and I cried until I could cry no more.

I felt so clean and forgiven, like my heart had literally been wiped clean of everything. It seemed like everything that had happened to me was now in the past. This was a fresh start, a new beginning in the right direction. I had experienced what I call a come about moment. "Come about" means to make a change in direction. It's what the captain on a ship would yell to his crew to get the ship ready to go a different route. And that's exactly what this experience did: Put me on a different route towards an amazing future.

As the summer began winding down, I asked the Watsons if they could adopt me. I loved being in a house with two parents, where we could talk about anything, from college to God to what kind of car I wanted to drive. Where I was able to enjoy being a kid. Where I didn't have to worry about bills being paid, utilities being shut off or arguments with my mom. I had my own room and bathroom. Where I had never even slept in a queen-sized bed or stepped foot in a brand new house. The Watson's house was my refuge.

Meet Cousin Anita

Cousin Anita was caramel-complected and tall with

beautiful silky hair. I thought she was kind of stern, but she was one of the most loving people you'd ever meet. She had been my doctor from a young age, but now I had begun to view her as my second mother. Every morning I would wake up and head downstairs to find her in the same spot on the couch studying her Bible. And each day I had more questions about God and life. We studied the Bible together and she would tell me all kinds of stories of people turning their lives around. I loved being around her; she had such a peaceful, calming spirit. I could tell her anything. She started to show me that motherly affection I was missing and longing for—that affection that my mother and I had lost. Cousin Anita knew about the relationship between mom and me, and therefore made it a point to speak my love language: Words of affirmation through communication. Every day we talked before and after we came home from work. She always knew when something was wrong, and frequently asked me what I was thinking and feeling. We communicated about everything, and she told me that I could be someone great.

One day I was laying on the floor watching a video on the internet. I was in awe of a woman who was speaking in a football dome encouraging women. The stadium was packed, and the event was broadcast across the nation to women in jail cells. You could literally feel the energy coming through the screen. It amazed me to see how one person's words had that much power to make an impact on that many people. I got excited just watching all these women come together and empower each other. The women on the screen were crying, hugging each other, celebrating, clapping and coming together as a united front. I picked up the computer to show Cousin Anita and said, "Look at this! Isn't this crazy!? This lady is speaking and encouraging literally thousands of women!" Cousin Anita looked at me and said, "and one day, you will too!"

I couldn't imagine that actually happening, but her words stayed with me. She believed that in spite of everything I had experienced, I had a story to tell. And sharing my story would influence, encourage and empower others. Maybe she had a point.

Back Down Memory Lane.

Cousin Anita sure was a stickler about cleaning! Not only did she teach me about having a clean heart, but also she taught me about having a clean house! Every Saturday, before I could go anywhere we had to clean the whole house. She laughed at my efforts to try and clean my bathroom. She would get down on hands and knees and show me how cleaning was supposed to be done. I even learned to pick weeds. One day I said to her, "Can't you guys just hire a maid to do this stuff?" Her response to me was, "Yeah, but I want you to learn to do all these things on your own. You will need these skills one day as an adult." Boy was she right! Nothing compared to when Cousin Anita's mom Nana would come to visit. During her stay I really had to make sure my room was spotless. Nana would come in, inspect my room, then teach me to how to make my bed the "right" way which included hospital corners and all.

One thing I appreciated about Cousin Anita was that she never talked bad about my mother/I took the stance that no matter what my mother had done or not done, no one and I mean no one could say anything negative about her. Cousin Anita respected my stance and never crossed that line. She knew all the things that my mother and I had been through and yet she would encourage me towards forgiveness. Although I protected my mother I was still very angry with her for not protecting me from Nelson. Cousin Anita would always tell me the truth about the importance of letting go of my past and working towards building a better future. Sometimes her words hurt, but then she would love up on me and make the truth a little easier to deal with. I had grown pretty defensive of motherly affection and tried my best to keep my guards up, but the love Cousin Anita showed me slowly tore them down.

One evening I spent the night at the house of one of the women from the church. We had such a great time talking about life and the future that I came home a little late the next day. Cousin Anita and I had missed our usual evening conversation so she took a few minutes before bed to say goodnight/By the time she stopped by my room I was already in my night clothes and reading in bed. She walked in the room like she normally would but this time she laid on my bed and said, "So tell me about your day." Immediately I sat straight up and my whole body stiffened. A million thoughts swirled in my head, "Why is she lying in the bed with me with her night clothes on? Is she going to do something to me? Why is she so close?" Every alarm went off in my body, and I was afraid of what was going to happen next. It had been years since my mother and I had shared a mother/daughter moment where we were physically close, e.g. hugging, lying down, or sitting on her lap. My mind flashed back to the last time an adult had gotten that close to me without my mother around. My emotions took a trip back down memory lane, to the day that Nelson had invited me to what I thought was a father/daughter conversation but ended up as some kind of sexual encounter. Here I was again getting ready to have another conversation with a parental figure in an intimate setting and I had no idea what to expect.

My thoughts raced as I tried to figure out what was getting ready to happen. Instinct told me to be prepared for the worst. Experience told me that even females could force you into sexual encounters. I thought about the things I had experienced but had never told anyone about. The times I attended sleepovers in elementary school with childhood best friends who wanted to play "house" and "pretend" that we were "husband and wife" (even though we were both girls). Friends who told me that part of playing house was laying on top of, rubbing up against and touching each other's private parts. I remembered the playmate who cornered me in her room and told me that I had to be "gay" with her as she forced her lips onto mine. My very first sexual encounters were with people whom I loved and trusted—people who were close to me and whom I considered my friends.

Heart beating, mind racing, my thoughts went back and forth between the past and the present. I tried my best to stay in the moment, but fear drew me back to the past. Minutes later, I snapped back to reality and realized that Cousin Anita just wanted to have girl talk. No ill intent, no sexual motive, just girl talk. It was in this moment that I began to really trust her. I learned that it was possible for someone to show healthy, intimate affection without it leading to a forceful encounter. I still stayed kind of guarded throughout the rest of our conversation but I appreciated the way she cared for me. She allowed me to be vulnerable with her and didn't take advantage of my innocence. We talked for a good hour before she said, "I'm glad you had a good time. I love you. Good night." It was a turning point I'll never forget

Meet Cousin Ron

Cousin Ron was caramel-complected, short, with a clean-shaven head. He sported a suit, tie and briefcase on a daily basis. He was my mother's blood cousin and my first boss. He was fully aware of all the trauma that my family had experienced and wanted to do something about it. He saw the same potential in me that my mother had when she was young. Potential to be creative, do well and attend a good college. He also saw the potential to end up in bad abusive relationships and settle for less. He saw me at the crossroads of a good life and a bad life. He knew that based upon my upbringing that the odds were stacked against me, so he did what so many others wouldn't. He intervened! He made it his business to shape and mold me so that I would be more likely to make good decisions for my life. He knew that if no one intervened, I would easily become another statistic. I would become another kid from the inner city who had the potential to be great but was never pushed into a fruitful destiny.

Cousin Ron shared knowledge and life skills with me every morning on our drive to work. He would ask me questions like what kind of career I wanted to have and what steps I needed to take to get there. He encouraged me to dream, to cast a vision for myself and make it a reality. He had me describe the type of house I wanted to live in and the car I wanted to drive right down to the make, model and color. Cousin Ron taught me how to write a check, open a bank account, make deposits and plans for my future. We went on bike rides together and spent time just thinking about how things in my life were going to be better. He encouraged me that my first goal was to be right with God and then consider all the other things I wanted out of life.

Cousin Ron was a lawyer by training so of course he

encouraged and encouraged and encouraged me to go to law school. Even with all his encouragement, my mind had always been on psychology, and more recently I considered going into the ministry. I knew that whatever I did, I wanted to help those who were hurting. Cousin Ron told me he would support me no matter which path I chose. He jokingly referred to our morning conversations as "lectures" and often thought I wasn't listening. He had no idea I was listening to every word. We had that father/daughter relationship that I always wanted but never had. I trusted him and didn't have to worry about him stealing from me, disappearing for days or being controlled by addictions like my biological father. I didn't have to worry about him abusing or handling me inappropriately like I did with Nelson. No one had ever talked to me about my future. I knew I was smart but no one had taken the time to encourage me to put my intelligence towards a career and make goals for myself. No one but Cousin Ron.

One morning I was in the mirror doing my hair for work when Cousin Ron walked to the doorway. He smiled and said, "Listen, there's no lecture for today, I just wanted to tell you that I love you." I didn't know how to respond. My father had never told me he loved me. My mother had said things like "I do this because I love you guys." But never spoken directly, "I love you." I paused and said, "ummm ok, uhhh, I love you too?" Cousin Ron laughed and said you look just like your mother with that expression. It's ok if you don't know how to respond." It felt good to hear those words but I wasn't quite sure what they meant. I knew what "I love you" meant in a relationship but not between a parent and child. It was another one of those moments where the Watsons made efforts to tear down the walls I had built against affection. I had no idea how to accept a father's love, and would later struggle in life with the ability to accept healthy love. Little did I know, these moments with the Watsons, along with several others, led me to a turning point in my life. Before meeting the Watsons I was a hurting little girl headed down the wrong path. I felt as though no one cared about me or loved me. I felt misunderstood and that my life would never get better. Being around the Watsons was different for me but I tried my best to be open to their love and guidance. If it weren't for them, I would have easily allowed my pain to keep me from reaching my full potential.

Surviving a Change in Direction

Oftentimes we become comfortable in pain and unhealthy patterns. Even if we are able to recognize that something or someone is not the best for us, we tend to find it difficult to break away for good. Going in a different direction often requires giving up something to reach our destination. That something is our comfort zone. If you never push past the boundaries that life or pain has created for you, you'll risk viewing your life from inside the walls and miss all the potential waiting on the other side. Taking a step in the right direction can be scary, but here are a few tips to help you with your journey. *Amen*

Survival Tips

1. Be Open Minded

Be open to the idea that the best direction for you to take may not be the most glamourous, popular or easiest route to your destination. It may be uncomfortable and unfamiliar, but if it's best for you it'll prove to be beneficial in the long run.

2. Avoid Assuming Everyone's Out to Get You

If you've been hurt before, it's easy to assume that everyone else will hurt you just like the people from your past. This is not necessarily true and prevents you from allowing people in who actually want to help and not hurt your process. Give people a chance and when they show you who they are, whether positive or negative, believe them.

3. Break out the Box

You don't have to fit the mold that pain has created around your life. Pain from the past usually teams up with fear and discourages you from making changes. Break out of the box by first committing to going in a different direction and then putting action behind your commitment. If you aren't able to taking a leap of faith, then walk. If you can't walk, then crawl. Just keep moving forward in the right direction.

EIGHT

When Love Hurts

Love at First Sight

My summer was going well and I loved being at the Watsons' house. They continued to pour into me daily and I was like a little sponge, soaking up all the knowledge, love and affection that I could get. Sadly, the love the Watsons showed me melted away only the tip of the iceberg of the love that I really desired: I wanted to be loved by a man. I wanted the romantic feelings of being wanted, appreciated and understood. As I mentioned before, finding a man was easy, but being in a relationship was not. I didn't really have a concept of monogamy and thought it best to talk to several guys at the same time because they could all satisfy different needs that I had, until I met Mike.

Mike was different than the guys I usually talked to. He

wasn't in the streets, didn't sell drugs and was a good student. Mike had a job, a car, went to church and could hold a good conversation. He was tall, dark and handsome. What more could a girl ask for? Immediately I fell "in love." He was only a grade ahead of me but 3 years older. Neither of us really cared about that because to us age was just a number. There were two problems though: (1) Mike kinda had a girlfriend and (2) He knew that I had a reputation for talking to a lot of guys (something he wasn't fond of). But we enjoyed each other's conversation so much that we decided to overlook our little "problems" and forge a relationship. We talked everyday about everything and hung out often. Eventually our hanging out so often led to becoming physically intimate, and this became our normal routine.

I had the attention of a lot of guys but Mike had mine. He listened to me, gave me advice about my problems and to make matters worse, he was super attractive. I grew more and more attached to him and was willing to give up my connections with every other guy if only Mike would ask me to officially be his. Mike and his girlfriend were on again off again and he wasn't quite ready to fully commit to me. He wanted the benefits of a relationship like spending time together and having sex, without the total commitment to each other. It hurt me but I put up with it just to keep him in my life. I felt like Mike understood me and I would never be able to find anyone better than him. I was blinded by love and willing to accept my handicap.

A Second Look at Love

I felt like that about Mike up until my experience at Vacation Bible School. We talked about love and relationships in our class and I discovered that there was a scripture in the Bible that defined love. It read, "Love is patient, love is kind. It does not envy, it does not boast, it is not proud. It does not dishonor others, it is not self-seeking, it is not easily angered, it keeps no record of wrongs. Love does not delight in evil but rejoices with the truth. It always protects, always trusts, always hopes, always perseveres. Love never fails." I had never heard love described in such detail. I had always thought love was just those butterflies you got in your stomach or a deep attachment to someone. I had also heard that love would make you do crazy things or put up with someone's mess even if they hurt you. I truly believed that jealousy, anger and arguing were the highlights of love. So of course I was shocked to hear all the amazing qualities and characteristics that defined it. Previously, the standard I had used to measure Mike's love was the fact that he had a girlfriend yet spent time with me and was intimate with me. In fact, I used this standard to measure love amongst most of the guys I talked to. I was known for talking to guys that had girlfriends. I thought that it was a true sign of love that they were in a relationship with someone else yet found time for me and unlike my relationship with Mike, I didn't have to be intimate with them. It made me feel special, wanted and appreciated. Even though I really was sitting second chair, my male friends made me feel like I was first because they took time to include me in their schedule. It made me feel loved.

But on second thought, I wondered if this new definition of love was really true. If it was, then that meant neither Mike nor any of the other guys I talked to really loved me at all. Heck, maybe I didn't love them either! I surely didn't exhibit most of these qualities, if any of them. So what was I feeling, then? During my second look at love, I realized that what Mike and I shared wasn't love at all. It was attachment and hormones. Truthfully, I was Mike's comfort, rebound, go-to girl when he and his girlfriend weren't on good terms. I was good enough to lie down with in private but not good enough to be his girlfriend in public. Our connection was self-seeking—which love is not. It was more about getting his needs met than truly forming a relationship. I decided I didn't want to be anyone's pillow or at their disposal for intimacy. I really wanted to change my life around, and I knew that meant distancing myself from Mike.

Love Hurts

During the summer I didn't contact Mike much, but I knew eventually I would. We had gradually stopped talking and he wasn't aware of my new changes. I called him one summer afternoon to update him on the new me. I was so excited to share everything I had been learning in church and at the Watsons' house. Mike had always encouraged me towards positive change and forgiveness toward my mother. So I knew he would be proud of me for beginning to turn my life around. I got Mike on the phone and began to share a few things that had happened since we'd last talked. After a few words, Mike told me that he was house sitting and wondered if I wanted to come "hang out." I told him I wanted to see him since I was at my mom's house for the weekend, but that I wasn't interested in doing "that." He agreed and told me to hurry and get dressed so he could come pick me up. I slipped on a short blue jean mini skirt and a tshirt with some flip flops. Those few minutes seemed like hours. I couldn't wait to see Mike and brag about my summer.

Mike picked me up and we headed straight to his neighbor's house. I talked the whole way about all the things I was learning and wanted to do differently in my life. Mike was happy for me, but he didn't really express his excitement the way I thought he would. We pulled up at his neighbor's house and he quickly got out of the car. I walked into the living room and sat down on the couch. I picked the conversation back up and continued to talk about my summer. I thought it was best for us to stay safe by just hanging out in the living room and catching up. Mike had another plan in mind. He said, "I'll be right back" and disappeared into the back hall. A few minutes later he came back and said, "Hey, want to watch a movie in the bedroom?" I responded, "Uhhh not really, I thought we were just gonna hang out here and talk." He said, "Yeah we could, but remember I owe you a massage because you gave me one last time." I sighed, "Yeah I guess you do owe me one." Reluctantly I followed Mike into the bedroom. He turned the TV on and plopped down on the bed. "Take off your shirt and relax," he said. I didn't really want to get undressed, but I figured a massage couldn't hurt. I lay down on my stomach and breathed another heavy sigh. I closed my eyes and tried to enjoy the massage. His big strong hands felt nice on my neck and tiny shoulders. Although I had preferred to just talk, it was nice to be around Mike again. I had missed him and always enjoyed our time together. I started to reminisce on the good times we had. With a smile on my face, I relaxed and took in the moment. I knew I was in good hands.

Just when I had started to relax, my moments of bliss were quickly interrupted. Mike flipped me over and straddled himself on top of me. He leaned in to kiss my neck and I said "Hey, no! I don't want you to do that. I'm not trying to get anything started." "Too late," he said. Mike pushed my skirt up. I quickly pulled my skirt back down and said, "No seriously Mike, I don't want to." He responded in his smooth baritone voice, "It's ok, I promise it'll be fine." "Yeah Mike, I know, but I really just don't want to," I said. I thought back to my Vacation Bible School Class and our discussion on celibacy. I was scared to publicly join the number that day of those who vowed to wait till marriage, but I made a promise in my heart: I wasn't a virgin but I truly wanted to wait until I got married to have sex again. I wanted to experience this love I had learned about, get married and then give myself away. Not like this, here in this room, at 15 years old, in some stranger's bed, with Mike who didn't love me.

I tried to get up, but Mike pushed me back down. "I'm serious Mike, I don't want to have sex," I said. "Ok, ok," he said. "Just let me go in for a sec, I'll be really quick." "No," I said, as I closed my legs and tried to get up a second time. Mike placed his hands on my knees and spread them apart. He pushed my skirt all the way up, pulled my underwear to the side and forced himself in me with no protection. I wanted to fight back, but I knew my 5'3", 110-lb frail body was no match for Mike, standing at 6'3" and weighing 230 lbs. I tried once more to close my legs and Mike forced them back open. I didn't want to have sex. Mike knew it, but he left me with no other option. We were in his neighbor's house, alone, no one else was around and he was my ride home. I couldn't get Mike off of me with words, and physically getting him off was impossible. I could've punched, kicked, screamed and yelled, but why would I do that? This was someone I loved, and it wasn't like he was raping me. He was just having sex with me and I didn't want him to, that's all...

So I lay there in disbelief as his gold chain dangled in my face. It was a charm with Jesus on the cross and a reminder that I had failed. I felt guilty and ashamed because I had broken my promise to God. I didn't say the celibacy vow out loud because I was afraid I couldn't keep it and if I couldn't keep it, God would be upset with me. My biggest fear had come true, against my will and it felt horrible. I felt disgusting, used, like a piece of meat being fed to a hungry dog. I had never told Mike 'no' before, and the one time that I did, how I thought and felt didn't matter. The fact that I wanted to remain celibate and just talk about my new life didn't matter. The fact that I didn't even want to have sex and had verbalized that, didn't matter. I was crushed but couldn't show it, because I figured if I did Mike would get mad and would no longer want to talk to me. I didn't want to risk losing my relationship with him. I loved him and he was there for me when I needed him.

So I stopped

I stopped fighting. I stopped trying to close my legs and asking him to stop. I stopped telling him no. It was clear to me at that point that Mike didn't really care about me. My 'no' meant nothing to him. He wanted to have sex, and at that moment that's all he cared about.

I lay there and let him continue his business.

I let him have my body while I went far away in my mind. I wanted the experience to be over, so I packed up my emotions and went somewhere pleasant. I imagined that I wasn't lying in that bed, and that Mike wasn't on top of me. I was on the beach enjoying the warm weather and the cool breeze blowing through my hair. The sand felt good between my toes as the waves splashed at my feet. There was no pain here. No force, no difficult emotions. Just peace and freedom.

Mike's grunting let me know he was almost finished, and I returned from my trip at the beach. He got up as if nothing had happened and apologized for the mess he had made on my skirt. I pulled my skirt down and asked him to take me home. I thought to myself, "I guess love really does hurt."

In the Name of Love

I couldn't believe what had just happened. It wasn't my first sexual encounter with Mike, but it was my first forceful encounter with him. I couldn't understand why he would be ok with having sex with me even though I told him I didn't want to. I questioned my true value to him. On the drive home, I asked myself, "Did I just get raped?" My thoughts were immediately counteracted by my preconceived notions about rape. Of course he didn't rape me. He didn't beat me up or hit me. I didn't have any bruises or anything. Plus, I knew him. People could only get raped by strangers, not by someone they knew. Not only did I know Mike, I loved him and we had been intimate before. It was just "different" this time, I told myself—and, I led him on. I did have on a mini skirt and cute undies, so he probably thought by the way I was dressed that I wanted it to happen anyway. If I didn't want anything to happen I should've just not went over there in the first place. I knew what he wanted when he said let's "hang out." So it was my fault for going over there. Plus, someone you know and love can't rape you anyways—right?

WRONG. WRONG and WRONG.

I was so wrong and didn't even know it. Mike had not violently taken advantage of me, but he did rape me. My experience with him is best described as date rape. Date rape is forcible sexual intercourse by an acquaintance during a voluntary social engagement in which the individual did not intend to submit to the sexual advances and resisted the acts by verbal refusals, denials or pleas to stop and/or physical resistance. I had asked Mike several times to stop and expressed that my intention was not to have sex. Despite my refusals, he ignored me and continued to make sexual advances. It wasn't until months later, sitting in a health class listening to a guest speaker that I realized that I had been raped

The speaker talked about how dating someone does not mean you have to have sex with them. She said if you're hanging out with your partner or date and they ask to have sex or insinuate sex, you have the option of telling them no. If you express that you do not want to have sex and they continue anyways with sexual acts, it is considered rape. I couldn't believe it: I had been raped. I really thought that what had happened between Mike and I was normal even though it left me feeling like crap. We didn't have sex together; he had sex with me without my permission. I didn't think it was rape, just that I didn't want to have sex and he did, so he won. I figured it happened to girls all the time, and I was no different. I thought if you loved someone you had to let them do whatever they wanted even if you didn't want them to—you know, in the name of love. I was in shock to learn that when I told Mike no, his sexual advances after that would qualify our experience as a rape.

Surviving When Love Hurts

As you read my encounter with Mike, you may find yourself thinking back to a similar experience you or someone you know had. Oftentimes we tend to have a stereotypical image in our head of what rape looks like. We assume that rape happens amongst strangers or that somehow the victim, especially if she is a woman, is to blame. That somehow she brought it on herself. All of these things are untrue. It is recognized amongst clinical professionals that the majority of rapes take place between people that know each other. Rape does not discriminate against clothing. Perpetrators can attack whether someone is dressed in lingerie or in a nun's habit. Whether you are a male or female, young or old, in love with the person or not, you're NO means NO. Any sexual act against your will is considered abuse. Anyone that tries to force you to go against your decision "in the name of love" or anything else is not someone who truly cares about your well-being. We say "love hurts," but it shouldn't have to. If your friend, partner or date truly loves you, they will respect you and your body by waiting until you are ready. Someone who doesn't respect your boundaries, space or will is not someone who loves you. If you're like me sitting in my health class, and upon reading this you've learned that you may have experienced rape or any other type of forceful act, please know that you are not alone. These next few tips may not take the pain away, but I hope they provide some comfort and guidance.

Survival Tips

1. Contact your local Rape Crisis Center or call the National Sexual Assault Hotline RAINN (Rape Abuse and Incest National Network) at 1-800-656-4673 for access to a range of free services including:

- Confidential, judgment-free support from a trained staff member
- Support finding a local health facility that is trained to care for survivors of sexual assault and offers services like sexual assault forensic exams
- Someone to help you talk through what happened
- Local resources that can assist with your next steps toward healing and recovery
- Referrals for long term support in your area
- Information about the laws in your area
- Basic information about medical concerns

2. Know that it was not your fault

It doesn't matter what you had on, where you were, if you were drinking or not, if you started out consenting and then changed your mind: If sexual acts were committed against your will, IT WAS NOT YOUR FAULT. People may try to tell you if you had not done this or said that then maybe it wouldn't have happened. Regardless of what you may or may not have done, if you said NO or if you were not able to give consent, it shouldn't have happened. Even if you had the right thing on, and were in the right place at the right time, there is no guarantee that the abuse would have been prevented.

3. Talk with someone who's safe

Rape is hard enough by itself to process; the last thing you need is someone blaming you for what happened. If you're not ready to talk to a professional, share your experience with someone who will have your best interest in mind. There's safety in numbers: Having at least one person who believes you and is willing to support you in your healing process can make a world of a difference.

NINE

With Determination

School Success

Over the summer, I had taken a turn in the right direction, but my experience with Mike was like driving into a pothole. If you've ever been to Cleveland, then you know we have some of the worst potholes in the world. I'm talking, you can totally jack your car up if you hit one of those things too hard. Your car may actually need a wheel alignment after driving into a Cleveland Crater. But as any Clevelander knows, you don't stop driving because there are potholes in the road. You keep going. You keep driving so you can get to your destination. And that's exactly what I did.

I was determined to be better and make a good life for myself. I thought my best chance at doing that was to live with the

Watsons. Being at their house was so peaceful and so amazing. I felt like for the first time in my life, I could actually be something, be someone who was important. I was growing and learning about myself and what I was capable of. I was learning how to forgive, to let go of the pain I had experienced and consider making a good future. Learning had always been my strong suit, and I wanted to learn more. So I asked the Watsons to adopt me. They were thrilled about my desire to stay with them, but since I was still a minor we had to get the ok from my mother. My mother and I talked, and she agreed that living with the Watsons was a good decision. Her strength and humility allowed her to see that the Watsons were able to help me grow in ways that she wasn't able to at the moment. Everything was set, and the Watson's proceeded to adopt me.

We started looking into the adoption process and were startled to find out that it could take months. It was the beginning of August and school was getting ready to start in a few weeks. The Watsons didn't want me to miss school being at their house, and I couldn't enroll in their school system until they had custody of me. So we all agreed that it was best to move back with my mom and attend my old school. Although I was not too thrilled to go back home, I was glad that I got to go back to my school. I had left Early College during my first year due to constantly getting into arguments with other female students over guys. Early College was predominantly populated by females and I guess there weren't enough males to go around. I was always in the center of drama about one boy or another. My mom thought it was best for me to transfer to my neighborhood school, John Marshall.

I loved Marshall. It was the school I wanted to go to all along. Both my brothers, Lee and Lem, went to Marshall and were well-liked and well-known. Just before the summer, I was finishing my second year there and was pulled aside one day by the guidance counselor. She went over my records and saw the changes they had made when I transferred in from Early College. Since Early College operated off of three quarters instead of four, halfway through my first year in high school I had already completed the 9th grade. By the time I got to Marshall I was supposed to be skipped up to the 10th grade, but their academic system wouldn't allow them to make me a 10th grader in the middle of the semester. Instead, they gave me a mixture of 10th grade classes, advanced classes and other classes where I could earn college credit. By my second year I was still in the 10th grade but had completed 11th grade classes. The guidance counselor met with me and said the school decided to give me two choices for the following academic year. Choice #1 was to remain in the 11th grade, come to school for half the day and then go to college for the other half of the day. Choice #2 was to be moved up to the 12th grade and graduate early. Before the summer I had chosen Choice #1, half high school and half college. I wasn't really ready to leave Marshall, and if I went to college for half the day my books and classes were paid for. I knew we didn't have money for me to go to college, so I figured this was the best route to go.

Upon returning to Marshall, I was shocked to learn that the school had made a decision for me: I got my schedule and saw that I had all 12th grade classes. I went to the guidance counselor and told her that there was some kind of mistake. She looked at me and said, "No, there's no mistake. You'll spend the first half of the year technically as an 11th grader. We got the ok to officially make you a 12th grader, when the semester is over. You're going to graduate early!" I left her office in disbelief— excited, but nervous. Graduating early was great, but I was only 15. What was I going to do with my life when I graduated?

Naw

Taking a Chance

By this time the cat was out of the bag and everyone knew my real age. Surprisingly, people didn't respond how I thought they would. My whole school career I was afraid to tell people how young I really was because I thought that they would make fun of me. In reality, it was just the opposite: People applauded me and celebrated me for being smart. Getting over that hurdle was all good, but what was I going to do being done with school at 15? No one was going to accept me into their college—I was too young—and how was I even going to apply for college? Both of my parents had gone to college, but they didn't finish. That was years ago; I'm sure the process has changed by now. How was my mom going to figure it out and get me registered? Most importantly, we didn't have any money or transportation. How was I going to get there?

These questions and so many others created fear and doubt in my mind. College was a great dream, but on the practical side it just didn't seem like a reality. I pushed the idea of college on the back burner and focused on taking a chance on a goal that I thought was more tangible: Winning homecoming. Since I was technically still in the 11th grade for the first semester, I wasn't eligible to run for Homecoming Queen against the 12th graders. So I aimed for the next best thing, which was Homecoming Princess for the 11th graders. I hung posters, passed out goodies and campaigned throughout the halls. Previously, I had depended on my male friends to buy my outfit and get my hair done. But this year was different. I was still working for Cousin Ron and at McDonalds, so I saved up my money to buy my own dress. The night of the dance I stood in the middle of the floor with the other candidates anticipating the results. They announced the runner up and I took a deep breathe. Come on, come on, just hurry up and say it, I thought to myself. And then the emcee said, "And our 2006 Homecoming Princess is…..Courtney Malone!!!" Whooh! I couldn't believe it. I won! All my hard work had paid off! I felt a sense of accomplishment and wondered if maybe, just maybe, I could apply this same amount of effort into applying for college.

Just Do It

My "maybe" became more of a possibility the day I met Nae Evans. From time to time, my school set up events where a representative from a college would come in and talk to certain students. Since I was in the advanced classes, I was on the list for those they "thought" would actually go to college. All of the students at the school lived in inner-city Cleveland, and the majority came from low socioeconomic backgrounds. Graduation alone was an accomplishment for many of the students, so college was seen on a whole different level of achievement. I walked in the event held in the school's library and was surprised to see a black female leading the session. Her name was Nae Evans. She was an admissions officer from Marietta College. The only other black female I knew with a stable career was Cousin Anita. Nae was in her 20s, professional and confident. I was intrigued and wondered what it took for her to earn that position. She obviously knew something I didn't, so I made sure to listen to her every word. She explained the ins and outs of Marietta and discussed options for financial aid. I knew about scholarships, but I thought you could get them only if you played sports. I had no idea that the government would give you money to go to college just based on the fact that your parents couldn't afford to pay tuition for you. Nae continued to talk, and stressed that there were even more financial aid opportunities for minorities that came from low-income households. I didn't know what a

minority was, but I didn't mind being one if it would pay for me
to go to college! *Lol*

Nae's presentation was inspiring, and I was ready to apply
for Marietta College. I literally wanted to tell her "Sign me up
right now!" It sounded so amazing! In spite of the excitement
though, a few issues still remained. I was still only 15, but by the
time I graduated I would be 16. We didn't have money to pay
for whatever financial aid didn't cover. Marietta was three hours
away, and we didn't have a car, so I had no way to get there. Seeing
that I had several major things working against me, I figured it
wasn't worth asking Nae for more information. But something
in me sparked, and a little voice said "Just Do It." Despite dismal
circumstances, a determination and curiosity rose in me to at
least see if there was a way for me to still apply. I walked up to
Nae after her presentation, introduced myself and told her my
situation. She responded with two questions: "Have you taken
your SAT/ACT? Are you going to graduate this year?" My
response to both of these questions was yes. Nae replied, "Well
then it doesn't matter how old you are; you can still apply and
be accepted!" "Really?" I asked. "Well, ok, but my parents don't
have a car, so I won't be able to go anyways," I said. Nae replied,
"Listen, don't worry about transportation. If you really want to
come visit Marietta I'll make it happen. I'll take care of it." And
that she did. She later sent me an email letting me know that
she had talked to the Director of Upward Bound (a program for

high school kids at the local college), who was already bringing a busload of kids to Marietta for a college visit. The Director was willing to allow me to come on the trip with them even though I was not a part of the program. Nae made sure nothing was going to keep me from getting to Marietta if I really wanted to be there. All I had to do was get downtown and get on the bus. Meals were also included on the trip at no cost to me. And just that easy, I was headed to visit the school I would soon grow to love.

Surviving with Determination

Oftentimes our dreams and ideas seem impossible or too far from reality. We'll tell ourselves "Well I can't do this because of this, that and the other. I'm too old or I don't know where to start." While all of these are valid concerns, they don't have to dictate your future. Fear is often the number one thing that holds many people back from accomplishing their dreams. Whatever your goals are, reaching them may not be easy, but it is possible. Here are a few tips on how to survive with an attitude that you can't be defeated.

Survival Tips

1. Believe in Yourself

It may be easy to fall into the pattern of the past and believe that if no one else in your family did what you want to do, then you probably can't either. Your family's accomplishments or lack thereof say nothing about you. If you think you can't then you won't, but if you think you can then you will. *amen*

2. Find Resources

Whether you're a high school student or an adult who has decided to go back to school, know that there are so many resources available to help you. Libraries, community centers, and local colleges often offer assistance with discovering your goals or choosing your career path. If all else fails, use the internet to search for what you need help with. There are tons of programs out there waiting on you to contact them.

3. Face Your Fears

The thing about fear is that it often doesn't go away until you address it head on. If you allow it to, fear can overwhelm you and hold you back from success. Ask yourself what is the worst possible thing that could happen if you decided to go after your dreams. Most people would answer, "I could fail." That may be true in some cases, but at least you could say you tried. At least you wouldn't have to live with regrets and what ifs. Even if you fail, you can always get back up and try again. And if your fear doesn't seem to go away, then do it afraid.

TEN

Free From Abuse

A Familiar Face

I applied to and was accepted into Marietta College at 15 years old. It was really happening. I—Little Ole Me—was going to college! I still had the rest of the year and the summer to prepare for my journey, but I was ready to go. I imagined getting out of Cleveland and being introduced to a new way of life. I wanted to be a professional—someone who had an important job, helping people and making good money. I felt like attending Marietta College was my first step in the right direction. But like any journey, smooth sailing is rare. In fact, most journeys include walking, climbing, running, or even crawling. There are often bumps in the road—and in some cases, potholes. They say for every mountain top experience there is also a valley. My life seemed to mirror just that. For every step I took forward, it felt like I was pushed two steps back. My feet had only just landed in the right direction when they were suddenly taken on a detour.

The signs told me to keep straight so I could get to my destination quickly and unharmed. For some reason, I figured I was familiar with the route and could handle the twists and turns of the road. I ignored the wrong direction sign though, and instead continued on my detour. My quiet drive was soon interrupted by a head on collision. The accident was so impactful; it left me damaged physically and emotionally. As I got out to see how bad my car was messed up, I realized I recognized the driver. I didn't know him personally but there was something that looked familiar about him. I checked his license plates and noticed the initials D.V. as he went through his wallet to grab his insurance card. I caught a quick glance at his license. I knew he looked familiar: First name Domestic, last name Violence.

Domestic Violence was an old family friend, whom I had never met personally but saw at several family events. The first time I remember seeing him was when my dad pushed my mom down the stairs. The next time was when Nelson hit my mother and left drops of blood on her wedding dress. He popped up often on my dad's side of the family. I remember a particular time he showed up at my cousin's house.

We were getting ready to head out the door when my older cousin and his girlfriend got into an argument. My cousin wanted her to do something and she told him it could wait until we got where we were going. My cousin didn't like her response and an argument ensued. The argument quickly got heated. I turned around to see what all the fuss was about and saw my cousin grab his girlfriend by the hair and pull her out the house. He dragged her down the driveway and delivered several punches to her face. She ended up with a face full of blood, swollen cheeks and two black eyes. And no one did anything. No police. No hospital. No jail time. She didn't want to go to the hospital because she didn't want to get my cousin in trouble. He was the father of her children, a drug dealer who made a lot of money and she depended on him financially. She wasn't going to ruin their relationship over a "fight." I felt so bad for her and for what she had to put up with. I liked her, and in fact she had saved my life—or at least saved me from some potential damage.

My cousin had gotten into a fight at the bar, and the guys he fought were coming to find him for payback. I was sleeping peacefully by the window facing the street when suddenly, my cousin's girlfriend pulled me down off the couch. I woke up alarmed and tried to get up off the floor. She hovered over me and said, "Stay down!" I looked out of the corner of my eye and noticed that all the other kids and adults were down on the floor, too. I thought to myself, "What the heck is going on?" Moments later, I got my answer as a bullet pierced through the window where I was previously laying. We were the target of a drive-by.

Fortunately, once the shooting stopped we were able to make it safely out the house and stayed somewhere else for the night. Violence had been around our family for so long that no one was surprised when DV showed up. I had previously only seen him in passing, but now I was getting ready to meet him face to face.

Beauty & The Beast

He was brown skinned, tatted, with a silky wavy cut. Urban-suburban gone church boy. His swag and style was on point. All the girls and some women wanted him. He showed up at church one day and immediately caught everyone's attention, including my own. After a few visits to the church, I found out his name was Sammy. Sammy approached me one day after church in the back hall. He asked my name and told me he found me attractive. We exchanged numbers and soon after started a relationship. Sammy came from a rough family and had a difficult childhood similar to mine. We connected right away and felt like no one else could understand us the way we understood each other. We both had family issues, emotional issues, were attractive and we went to church. We were the perfect pair. There was something beautiful about our relationship because we came from similar backgrounds, but there was also something beastly.

Shortly after we started dating, I began to notice that Sammy was a little controlling. He lived on the eastside and I stayed on the west side, so during the school week we didn't see each other often. On days that we didn't see each other, Sammy would often ask for my schedule for the day. He wanted exact times of what I would be doing, who I would be with, where I was going and how long I was going to be there. It seemed ok at first until one evening I went to the mall with a female friend. I told Sammy I was going to hang out and would call him when I got back. My friend and I decided to go to dinner and then going to the mall, so our hangout time ended up being a little longer than what I had initially told Sammy. When I got home and called him, he was pretty upset. I told him that we went to dinner before the mall, which is why I came home later than I initially had said. He had several questions for me including, what stores did you go to and how much time did you actually spend at the mall? He said that he had called certain stores in the mall to make sure I really was there. I thought it was kind of weird that he had called the mall but at the same time I thought it was cute that he would "check on me." Crazy, but cute. Plus, you did crazy things when you were in love—right? Somehow I had quickly forgotten my new-found definition of love that stated: Love always trusts...

Sammy's craziness continued in arguments. He would often talk down on me and tell me he could have any girl he wanted, and that I should be happy he chose me. I figured he had a point: All of the girls I knew thought he was amazing and wanted a chance with him. He was often passed notes in church from girls offering their "services" to him. Sammy had even charmed some of the adult women. It seemed as though everyone wanted a piece of him. He would tell me I didn't look like the girls he usually talked to. He showed me pictures of girls who lived in the suburbs with wealthy parents and "good hair." He liked women that were foreign or had a Middle Eastern, Hispanic or Asian look. I had the light skin, slim body, and slanted eyes, but not the foreign hair; my hair was thick and wavy, nowhere near straight. Sammy made fun of my hair during arguments. He called me bald head and ugly, and frequently said I looked like someone who had Down's Syndrome. Even though I had a head full of shoulder length hair, it wasn't straight enough, long enough, or silky enough for Sammy. He often compared me to other girls and made me feel like crap. Even when we weren't arguing, he had no problem telling me how he saw a girl with a certain hairstyle that he knew I couldn't pull off and how much he wished I could wear my hair like that. It was obvious that in our relationship, Sammy thought he was the Beauty and I was the Beast. My self-esteem went out the window, and I depended totally on Sammy to make me feel good.

I knew that Sammy thought I was the scum of the earth, but for some reason I didn't want to end the relationship. Surprisingly, neither did he. So I did what I knew best, and looked elsewhere to get my needs met. I started talking again to my previous male friends, and Sammy was livid when he found out. Sammy had gotten kicked out of his house and had nowhere to stay. He would sleep at a friend's house or sometimes in the park. My mom would let him come over and stay sometimes so he wouldn't have to sleep outside. One day, Sammy was in the basement washing clothes. I was in my room and figured since he was downstairs I'd call a male friend for some encouragement. Sammy heard my conversation through the vent and came upstairs heated. We started arguing and he reached for the box that held my prom tickets. Sammy said, "If you want to talk to other people, fine. Take someone else to prom then!" He grabbed the box, pulled out the tickets and ripped them up right in my face. I watched as a million little pieces fell to the floor. Sammy had gotten a job and taken the little money he had and paid for our prom tickets. My aunt had bought me a $400 dress. My hair, makeup and nails were going to be paid for and everything else was ready to go. The tickets were $100, and I knew I didn't have the money to pay for them. The school only had a certain amount of tickets and they were first come first serve. Prom was just a few weeks away and I was pretty sure that the tickets were sold out. My only chance at attending prom was literally snatched away in seconds.

Eventually, the arguments between Sammy and I became so frequent and intense my mother asked Sammy to leave and not come back to her house. Right after an argument, I was in agreement with this, but as my anger faded I'd miss Sammy and want him to come back. My mother forced me to break up with him and forbade me from talking to him. But like any teenager who thinks she's in love, I longed for him. Somehow he made me feel horrible and loved at the same time. I wanted his attention because I knew that he could easily give it to someone else—and I didn't want that.

The Beast Erupts

Shortly afterward, Sammy got a car and wanted to show me what he bought. He told me to sneak out of the house so he could take me for a ride. We jumped in his beat up Jeep and drove down to the lake. We started talking and things seemed to be going well. The conversation quickly took a turn as we discussed who had our attention since our "break up."

If I had told Sammy that I was interested in anyone else, it would have caused an argument. I didn't want to ruin the moment, so I told Sammy I wasn't talking to anyone. He knew I was lying and reached over to grab my phone. I closed my fist and instead of grabbing my phone, Sammy grabbed my hand. He tried to pry my fingers from my phone and get me to loosen my grip. I asked him to stop, but he continued; he was determined to get the phone out of my hands. So he reached over while putting his weight on me, and tried to pull my hands once again. "Sammy, get off of me," I said, and pushed him back. He lunged at me, but before he could get to me, I punched him in the face. He punched me back and we started dishing out blows. We got out of the car swinging and stopping at nothing to make sure the other person was hit. Sammy grabbed the windshield wiper fluid out of his trunk and tried to pour it on me. As the fluid splattered on the ground I looked down and noticed I had on boots. I figured if Sammy continued to come after me, I would kick him and that would stop the fight. He lunged once more, so I kicked him in the face. Sammy threw a few more punches, then jumped back in the car and locked the door. I didn't have a way home, and I had dropped my phone under the car during the fight. Sammy said, "I'm leaving you here. Find your own way home." I walked up to the window to try to persuade him to take me home, or at least to let me use his phone so I could call for a ride. Sammy rolled down the window as if he were going to talk to me. Instead, he spit in my face, backed the car over my phone and drove away. My phone was smashed, and I had no way to get home.

I noticed a few people walking along the lake, and I went to them to ask to use their phone. I called my mother and told her what happened. She walked several miles to get me from the lake and called the police on her way. My mother and the police showed up to take me home, but no charges were pressed. *(new)*

The Beast had erupted in our relationship. But because he was a familiar face, I went back for more. After the fight, Sammy and I apologized, laughed about it and continued to talk. He made light of the fact that I could fight and had blackened his eye and chipped his tooth. We thought we were crazy in love.

Crazy yes. Love, no. Sammy knew that I would be graduating soon and leaving for college. He wanted to make every effort to still stay attached and control my every move. Sammy was aware that I couldn't afford to buy another phone after he broke the one I had. His next move of control was to buy me a phone and pay the bill. But of course this came with several stipulations: No one else besides family could have my number, because it was in his name. He had access to the bill to make sure I didn't call anyone outside my family. I also had to answer every time he called, and the phone had GPS so he could track me wherever I was. I was hesitant, but agreed because I needed a phone. I also wanted to prove to Sammy that despite our problems, I wanted our relationship to work.

Sammy saved up enough money and got a place of his own. I was excited for him, but it also shot my insecurity through the roof. I wasn't allowed to see Sammy, so any visits had to be done without my mother's knowledge, which was kind of hard. Even though Sammy lived around the corner, I couldn't see him as much as he would have liked me to. I figured if I couldn't see him, then he'd talk to someone who could. Sammy was good at telling me he had company or was going to have company. This made me mad, but it also made me find a way to come see him. He knew how to manipulate me into getting what he wanted. An unexpected trip to Sammy's apartment was prompted by him telling me that a girl I knew from school was coming over. She was pretty and slim, with long hair just liked Sammy liked it. I was enraged, jealous and wanted to stop this visit. I told Sammy I was on my way over and that "she" better not be there when I got there.

Knocked Off My Feet

I walked down the street and knocked on the door to Sammy's apartment. He pretended that he didn't want me to come in. He cracked the door and said, "She's not here. She just left." I wasn't sure if he was lying or not so I asked to come in. Sammy said, "Seriously she's not here." I leaned on the door and pushed my way in. Sammy was telling the truth; she wasn't there. I questioned whether she ever was there or if he had just said that to get me to come over. We started talking but our talking quickly turned into an argument. The argument escalated into another fight.

Sammy grabbed me by my hair and smacked my head into the wall. I screamed for him to let go of my hair, and after a moment he did. I grabbed the iron and threw it in his direction. It barely missed him. I looked for something else to throw. My eyes fell on his kitty litter box. I went to reach for it, but I wasn't quick enough or strong enough. Sammy grabbed the kitty litter box before I could and dumped it and its contents out on my head. The weight of the box knocked me to the ground and Sammy picked me back up. He pushed me out of his apartment and into the parking lot. I tried to walk away and told him I didn't want to fight anymore. I started feeling dizzy and I really just wanted to get home.

Sammy walked behind me taunting and yelling names at me. I asked him to call my mom because I felt like I was getting ready to pass out. Sammy didn't believe me. He told me he was going to tell everyone at church how crazy I was and they would believe him because they liked him better than they liked me. As he talked, my head continued to spin and I felt like I couldn't walk any further. I laid down in someone's front lawn and told Sammy to go get help. This time Sammy finally realized that I was telling the truth and something was wrong. He picked me up, called my mom and carried me the rest of the way home. My mom rushed home and found me sitting on my bed. I stood up to tell her what happened but passed out in her arms. Sammy had literally knocked me off my feet.

It turned out that Sammy hitting my head against the wall had given me a concussion. My previous fights with Sammy had resulted in bruises, scratches, black eyes and cuts, but never a concussion. Unfortunately, this wasn't my last encounter with Sammy—or Domestic Violence. My relationship with him continued on for a few more months and didn't end until I went off to college. I was able to talk to the school and still go to prom. But as a result of my relationship with Sammy, I lost so much more. My self-esteem was gone, I didn't think I was physically attractive anymore and I truly believed that no one would want me. I felt like damaged goods and that I would never find anyone better than Sammy.

Surviving Free from Abuse

Oftentimes when we hear of domestic violence situations, we tend to say, "If the situation is that bad, why don't they just leave?" Leaving is easier said than done. In fact, most women leave and come back to a domestic violence relationship at least seven times before they leave for good. Men can experience domestic violence as well, but they typically don't report it due to embarrassment and fear of not being believed. People stay in abusive situations for multiple reasons, such as: The abuser has threatened to harm them if they leave; They are concerned about being harassed or stalked; Children may be involved; The abuser may have financial power and control; Or the person being abused simply has low self-esteem, has seen people in their family abused and believes he or she can't do any better. Whatever the circumstances, leaving is difficult. But surviving free from abuse is possible. Here are a few tips to show you how.

Survival Tips

1. Call it for what it is

Most people have a hard time acknowledging that the relationship they're in is abusive. Force, control, physical fighting, harassment, isolation, threats, extreme jealousy, irrational suspicions or anything similar are not part of a healthy relationship. These characteristics are not normal, and should be considered red flags and signs of an abusive relationship. As embarrassing as it is, acknowledging that the relationship is abusive is the first step to getting help. *amen*

2. Avoid Assumptions & Excuses

Making assumptions and excuses tends to keep both women and men in unhealthy relationships. The person being abused tends to assume that the abuse won't happen again or that their abuser will change. Research shows that most men who are physically abusive do not change—not because they can't, but because they tend to have no reason to because their behavior is not challenged by their partner. Some men do change, but it takes a lot work on their part, and usually collaboration with a good therapist. The abused also tend to assume that they can't or won't find anyone better. This is just fear, and not at all true.

There is someone out there who will love you and treat you the way you deserve—and if not, it's better to be single than to be abused. Avoid making excuses for the abuser and thinking "if I just did this right" or "if they were just able to do this" then the abuse would stop. Domestic Violence is not about what you did or didn't do, it's about power and control. The abuser's behavior is not your responsibility; you are not at fault for how they treated you. Lastly, avoid the excuse that "your situation is not as bad as someone else's so it doesn't need intervention." Even if your partner never knocks you out, if they harass you, stalk you, threaten you or make frightening gestures, this is still considered Domestic Violence, and it still needs to be addressed.

3. Get Help

People often fear leaving because they may lose everything in the process: Finances, shelter, transportation, a companion, etc. There are resources that can assist with leaving and getting back on your feet. Call your local Domestic Violence Shelter or the National Domestic Violence Hotline at 1-800-799-7233.

From Victim to Survivor

ELEVEN

When You Think You Can't

Roadblocks

My relationship with Sammy had taken me on a dangerous detour, but thankfully it was just that: A detour and not my final destination. I graduated from John Marshall High School at the age of 16—the youngest in my class—and prepared to go to college. I had been accepted into Marietta College and couldn't wait to get out of Cleveland. Although Marietta was ready to welcome me as a first-year student, there were still a few hurdles I had to jump over for college to become a reality. Marietta had offered me an amazing financial aid package, but it did not cover the total cost of tuition. The other issue that presented itself was that I didn't have much money to buy the necessities for my dorm. My mom was working at Target at the time so she was able to get a few things discounted, but I was on my own to buy the rest of the things I needed. Even if those things were taken care of, I still had one big issue: Marietta was 3 hours away, and we had no car and no way to get there.

Any good survivor knows that where there's a will, there's a way. I was determined to get to college. I wasn't going to let these roadblocks prevent me from my future. So I organized a going-away party and asked people to bring gifts and cash. I received a few dollars as graduation gifts, and racked up enough money to buy the necessities for my dorm room. One problem solved, two more to go. The Billing Department called my mother the week I was supposed to go to school. They told her that I still owed $1500, and I could not report to school without this bill being paid. My mother had applied for the federal PLUS Loan, but was denied. All loans and financial information had to be in my name. I knew there was no way we could come up with $1500 in just a few days. I was bummed out because I knew I was literally just $1500 away from my way out.

I told myself, "Courtney, you've come too far, and it's too late to give up now." I got down on my knees and said, "God, please work everything out. I really want to go to school. You know I can't afford it, but I know you can make it happen. Amen." The next day, the school called and said there had been an error in the bill, and I no longer owed the $1500! They authorized me to report to school later that week! My mother had been trying her hardest to find transportation for me and finally a friend of hers came through. Her friend had a van and offered to drive my family and my stuff to college. Everything had worked itself out. This 16-year-old little black girl from Cleveland was now headed to one of the top ranked private colleges in the Midwest.

On my drive to Marietta I began daydreaming about how life in college would be. I didn't want to drink, party or stay out late. Heck, I was only 16; I couldn't even see a R-rated movie by myself. My thoughts shifted toward making a better life for myself and my family. I knew that once I got my degree I would come back to Cleveland and help other people change their lives. So many of the people I went to high school with didn't go to college, and had no idea that they were missing out on a whole different world. When we arrived, my family helped unpack my stuff. As we unloaded our things, I noticed stares from some of the other students, but I didn't pay them much attention. My mother and I stood in my dorm and hugged each other goodbye. It was a bittersweet moment. On one hand, I was sad to leave her; but on the other hand, I couldn't wait to truly be on my own. My family left shortly after, and my life at Marietta College began.

Life at Marietta

On my first day of class, I walked in and was surprised to see that I was the only black girl in almost all my classes. Growing up in inner-city Cleveland, I was used to being around people of different races—but it was obvious that my classmates were not. As I walked through the door to my First Year Seminar

Experience class, I noticed the same stares I had gotten upon moving in. I checked my shirt and thought maybe I had spilled something on myself and that's why they were staring at me. I felt their glares all throughout the class, and couldn't wait for an opportunity to say something. The professor came to the point in class where she allowed us to address anything that was on our minds. I raised my hand and said, "How many of you have ever been in class with a black person?" The professor seemed shocked by my question, but allowed the class to answer. About 5 students raised their hands. I went on to explain how I had noticed their stares and that it wasn't polite. I told them I wasn't trying to make them uncomfortable, but I would appreciate it if they stopped staring at me. Ha! And that they did. The professor praised me for my courage and emphasized the importance of diversity. There were definitely other races on campus including international students, but "we" the black kids were few. We came together at least once a day to share our experiences and hang out in the lounge with the coolest brother on the campus: Mr. Taran McZee.

Meet Taran

Taran McZee was the Multicultural Affairs Director and Advisor for Charles Sumner Harrison (CSHO), a multicultural student organization. I first met Taran during the trip that Nae Evans organized for me to visit Marietta College. Taran was tall, brown-skinned and had a personality that was out of this world. He was super charismatic, hilarious and had a heart for all his students. Besides Cousin Ron, he was the only other black man that I had ever seen dressed nicely all the time. As a freshman it was good to see a familiar face on campus. Taran's office was connected to a lounge where most of the minority students hung out. There weren't many of us, so we all hung together as a family. The lounge was where we'd watch BET, talk about our experiences in class, receive advice from one another, figure out how we were going to get our hair done—oh, and argue like cats and dogs. For the black female students, trying to figure out how we were going to get our hair done was a big thing. The salons around town didn't know how to work with our hair, so we gave each other tips on how to do it ourselves. We later discovered a hair school who was able to help us out as well. Taran was responsible for bringing us together, like a family. He was the dad, big brother, mentor, advice-giver and problem-solver all in one. He put on events that we enjoyed, and made us work together on projects as a team. We all appreciated his efforts to make us feel at home.

Every day during lunch, I headed for the lounge to check in with the other students, use the computer or to talk with Taran. We could talk about anything—from boys, to things going on at home, and even spirituality (although we had a few disagreements in this area). Taran was from Flint, Michigan, and if you know anything about Flint you know that it's one of the most violent, crime-stricken cities in the country. So he understood with ease where most of us with rough lives were coming from. But Taran had made it out! He had 2 degrees, a good job, a beautiful fiancée and lots of students who loved him. He sat in a position that many of us looked up to and desired to be in one day. Through our daily conversations, Taran began to see potential in me that I didn't see in myself. He encouraged me to believe that I didn't have to be a product of my environment. He said I could make better decisions, even at 16, that would lead to the life I wanted for myself. Taran mentioned that he thought I would be a great candidate to run for an Executive Board position for CSHO. He also encouraged me to run for the Minority Affairs Commissioner (someone who spoke on behalf of black, Asian, and Hispanic students) position on Student Senate, so I did. I received both positions, and began to make an imprint on campus.

Taran gave all of us lessons on life and professionalism. He would get on the boys who sagged their pants and the girls who didn't do their hair in the morning. He had a rule that we could not wear pajamas to class or he would talk about us the whole day. He wanted us to begin to prepare our minds for the workplace. Taran continued to pull out the potential in me and introduced me to the other "big wigs" on campus, as I liked to say. I attended meetings with the Dean of Student Affairs, The Provost and The President of Marietta College. Taran wanted me to get as much exposure to professionalism and networking as

I possibly could. He not only cared about my professional well-being but also my personal good.

My cousin Carolyn suddenly passed away while I was at school. I left campus and went home to be with my family. During breaks I usually caught a ride with one of the other students from Cleveland. Since this was during the regular school week, I had no way to get back to school when it was time to come back. I had spent all my money on a one-way Greyhound ticket home, and couldn't afford to come back to school. I called Taran and told him that maybe it was just better that I leave school for a while to be with my family. I was tired of struggling financially, and I wanted to be able to take care of my family. Being in school, I couldn't work a full time job and also take care of things at home. Although Taran understood my position, he wouldn't let me quit school. Without hesitation, he bought me a Greyhound ticket to come back to campus. It was a moment I'll never forget.

Taran believed in me. Although he knew it was difficult, he challenged me to finish the race. He was well aware of the challenges some of the inner city students faced when they went home—poverty, bad neighborhoods, gangs, violence—and did whatever he could to make sure we returned. Some time after returning to school, Taran sat me down and talked with me about my future. At 16 years old I had made the Dean's List and was already ahead in my General Education Classes. The college credits I earned in my advanced high school classes transferred over and allowed me to receive credit for three of the General Ed classes. Taran said if I stuck with the same major in Psychology and minor in Religion, it was likely that I would graduate early. The other thing he asked me to consider was applying for the Leadership Program.

The Leadership Program was one of the highlights of Marietta College. It was a prestige program that taught students to be global leaders, whether in politics, business or non-profits. Students had opportunities to attend national conferences, travel abroad, and participate in a partnership with Harvard University. Only the cream of the crop was accepted, and Taran felt as though I had what it took to apply. I hesitated because I didn't think I could do it. I didn't think I was as smart as the other students, but I applied anyway.

I was accepted into the Leadership Program!

I Think I Can, I think I Can...

I was the only black student in the entire program—and of course in all my leadership classes. At this point I had gotten used to that. But there was something else that bothered me: These kids knew more than I did. Academically I could hold my own, but they knew more about politics, world leaders, world events—things I had no clue about. Most of the students came from wealthy suburban families, whose parents had great careers and did important things in the world. And me? I knew nothing about that life. I had spent high school in bad relationships, working two jobs, worried about bills not getting paid, lights getting cut off and trying to figure out how I was going to buy clothes and shoes. I didn't care what was going on around the world. I was just trying to survive in my own world. Feeling like I was at a disadvantage was bad enough; what made me really uncomfortable was that the leadership classes were not lecture-based. They were discussion-based, meaning that you had to talk about these topics, not just take notes and listen to the professor talk. How in the world was I going to talk about these things when I had no idea what was going on outside of Cleveland, OH?

My Leadership professor, Dr. McManus, noticed that I never gave my opinion during discussions. He'd often ask for my thoughts, and I'd often reply "no comment." I did well in classes where we learned skills like parliamentary procedure, how to facilitate a meeting, rules for doing business in other countries, etc. But when it was time to discuss current events, I had nothing to say. Sometimes I just didn't know what to say; other times I got upset about the topic. One day we were discussing an incident on the news where white police officers had arrested a black man because they didn't believe he lived in his house. He had forgotten his key and was going through the window, and because it was a nice house, the officers thought he was trying to break in and arrested him. He had tried to tell them that he lived there and they did not even give him the opportunity to show his ID to prove his residency. President Obama made a statement about the incident and called the officers "Stupid." The class was asked to share their thoughts on the incident. All of my classmates seemed to think that the officers were right in what they did and Obama was wrong and unprofessional to call the officers stupid.

I sat in class in disbelief. I wanted to tell each and every one of them off. I wanted to go off about how the incident was based on racism, and there was nothing wrong with Obama calling it like it was: "Stupid." I twisted my face up, rolled my eyes, smacked my lips—but remained silent. Dr. McManus was drawn to my expressions and asked me to step outside the classroom. He said, "Courtney, I know that this is a sensitive subject for you, but you need to speak up. How will they ever know a point of view different from their own if you don't say anything?" "But they sound so stupid," I said. "They all live in little bubbles in their perfect little worlds. They don't understand anything about racism or struggles. They are the ignorant ones." "I understand where you're coming from," he responded, "but how will they know if you don't educate them? You bring a unique perspective to this class. Now, take a deep breath and articulate your point intelligently. I know you can do this. You got this." He opened the door and we headed back into the classroom. Seconds later he said, "Courtney, what do you think about this?" My heart was pounding so loud I could hear it beating out of my ears. I swallowed hard and looked at Dr. McManus for reassurance. He nodded his head and said, "You got this." I was afraid to share my point of view because I thought the other students would think I was stupid or take pity on this poor little black girl. I took a deep breath and told myself, you can do this. I begin to explain my point of view. I asked if they or anyone they knew had experienced something like this, and if they did how would they want others to respond. The class was silent, and Dr. McManus emphasized my point. He thanked me for sharing and continued on with the class.

Dr. McManus continued to work with me on how to share my point with the class without getting upset. He taught me how to sit through difficult conversations and challenge my peers to be more open-minded. I met with the Dean of the Leadership Program, Dr. Perruci, and he was intrigued to learn about my story and progress. I stood out in the program, and Dr. Perrucci often asked for my feedback. He wanted to know why I thought most of the minority students didn't even try to apply for the program. He also asked about the challenges I had to endure to get to college and praised me for overcoming them all. I was selected out of several students to attend a National Leadership Conference in Austin, Texas. I really wanted to go, but could not afford the cost. I went to Dr. McManus and told him my dilemma. He helped me find scholarship money to cover most of the cost and I only had to come up with about $50 out of pocket.

I expressed my gratitude and excitement, but also my fear. I had never flown on a plane, I didn't know how to book a flight and I couldn't remember how to write a check. Dr. McManus told me not to worry. He booked my flight and showed me how to write a check for the $50.

Dr. McManus, Dr. Perruci, and Taran continued to invest in me and push me to go beyond the boundaries I had created for myself. Their encouragement, time and efforts helped me switch my thinking pattern from I Can't to I Can. And I did. I got to know my professors and discovered that Marietta had some of the best teachers around. They all were extremely helpful and supported me on my journey to success. Bonding with the students and staff increased my confidence to connect with others who were different than me. Every now and then someone would make a racist comment, but I learned to take them in stride. I had someone from the community ask where I was from and how I could afford to go to Marietta. Someone else asked me what country I was from and said I needed to go back to China. These types of comments only fueled my desire to educate my peers on the importance of discovering and embracing diversity. I applied for several opportunities on campus where I would have a voice, and I was accepted to them all. I became an Orientation Leader, the Minority Affairs Commissioner for Student Senate and CSHO, served on the Women's Program Committee, became a Resident Assistant (didn't stay on for long), and Created a

Diversity Program that was used in Freshman Orientation. I won 2 awards in the Religious Studies Department and was inducted into Psy Chi, the International Honor Society of Psychology. During the week I worked a few hours for Taran in the lounge, at a daycare after class, and at the mall on the weekends. I also picked up work-study hours throughout the week. I bought my first car and took trips home as often as I could.

Back at home, I worked at Target on breaks and sent money to my little brother when I had a few extra dollars. I could've easily gotten wrapped up in what was going on at home and that my family was struggling. But I knew I had to stay focused and finish my degree at Marietta. Close to graduation, I picked up an internship with the Washington County Children and Family Services. I immediately fell in love with helping kids and families. I knew that I wanted to be a counselor, and my experience in my internship further affirmed my desire. As my final year approached, I realized I had only one semester left. Taran was right: I was going to graduate early! On top of that, the scholarships, grants and awards I received covered my tuition for two and a half years. I ended up taking out loans for the cost of only one year of tuition. I received my Bachelor's Degree with Honors in Psychology, and a Certificate in Leadership, at the age of 19. Not only did I learn to think I Can, I Did. I made it! I survived college and managed to graduate early again!

Surviving When You Think You Can't

I grew to love my college experience at Marietta, but I had to jump through several hurdles to reach my destination. Whether you're attending a college where you are the minority, or you're trying to accomplish something that you deem impossible, don't count yourself out. Maybe you've experienced so much pain in life that you've trained yourself to think that you'll never be happy or you'll never overcome your pain. Even if the weight of the world is on your shoulders, there is still hope that you can accomplish your goals. If you're tired of fighting and need a break, then rest. But don't quit. Surviving takes work. Here's how you can adjust to your environment.

Survival Tips

1. Get Connected

I know this may be difficult, but the only way you will change your thoughts is by plugging into positive people, places or activities. Connect with a group, church, life coach, counselor or attend empowering uplifting events. When you constantly hear "You Can," eventually you will believe it and begin to Do.

2. Change Your Thinking

Our thoughts become our feelings and our feelings become our actions. If you think you can't, then you won't. But if You Think You Can, then You Will. If it's not in your mind first, then it won't be in your life. Think it, Speak It, Do It. Just like The Little Engine That Could, begin to tell yourself "I Think I Can, I Think I Can" and you'll start trekking up the mountain in no time. For more help with changing your thought process, check out the From Victim to Survivor Workbook.

3. Ignore Comparisons

It's easy to think you can't when you feel you don't have what others have. Of course the grass looks greener on the other side. But the truth is, the grass can be greener wherever you water it.

The presence of someone else's gifts does not mean the absence of your own. You were created with unique abilities, gifts and talents too. Throw comparisons in the trash, and learn to be comfortable with who you are—and who you are not.

Amen

TWELVE

Life After Death

Death is Necessary

Well, Friend, I made it. I survived Against the Odds, When Things weren't what They Seemed, In Second Place, As the Underdog, When It was Time to Go. I survived On Purpose, A Change in Direction, When Love Hurt. I survived With Determination, Free from Abuse and When I Thought I Couldn't. I Survived being the child of a drug-addicted parent, seeing my family members beat up by their spouses, a drive-by, poverty, sexual abuse, rape, physical abuse, and going to college as a minority. I survived—and You Can, too! We were all created with an internal instinct to survive, to keep living when everything else around us and in us tells us to die. The only thing in us that needs to die is the Victim Mentality and all the baggage that it brings with it.

The Victim Mentality told me that I was not good enough. It said that I was broken and damaged, and that I would always be that way. It told me that my mother didn't love me, and that I could use people to try to fill my voids. The Victim Mentality told me that dysfunction was the norm and that I wouldn't recognize a healthy relationship to save my life. It said that I would never be ok, and that I couldn't break the cycles of destruction in my life because no one else in my family did. The Victim Mentality kept me embarrassed, ashamed, guilty, fearful, sad and feeling empty. But I discovered that the only way for me to truly live was to die to this way of thinking. I used the survival tips mentioned in this book and the exercises in the From Victim to Survivor Workbook to overcome my trauma with truth. I discovered that the negative things I believed about myself were lies. I allowed the lies I believed based on my experiences to keep me a prisoner for long enough. Through encouragement from others, therapy and prayer I discovered I had the ability to change my thinking and consequently change my life. As painful as the process was, I realized that there truly is Life after death. As the Victim in me died, The Survivor came Alive.

The Life of a Survivor

Surviving is a process. It doesn't happen overnight and it

doesn't happen alone. Without the help of amazing people along the way—like the Watsons, Taran, Martha Robinson, Jackie Douglas, Dr. McManus, Dr. Perruci—I would have remained a Victim. My wounds were deep, long-lasting, and my healing has taken place over time. My relationship with my parents was restored. My cycles of dysfunction and abuse were broken. I found my voice, and discovered that I was passionate about helping others transition from Victims to Survivors. I met my husband Mario and became the mother of two beautiful girls, Faith and Taylor. Healing, Happiness and Wholeness captured my eye years ago, and I've committed to reaching and maintaining these beautiful virtues. The survival of the fittest, pretty much, sums up my life experiences. Learning to survive was necessary to get to where I am today. Little did I know that learning to survive was only the first part of my story. Now it was time to THRIVE!

Dear Survivor

You made it! I knew you could do it! Reading through this book, you may have laughed, cried, pondered and reflected. Diving in to my story may have caused some of your own painful experiences to resurface. If so, I encourage you to find someone to talk to in order to process what you're feeling. Being a survivor doesn't mean that you will never need help again. It means that you have first recognized that there is a wound, and have taken healthy steps to heal. While you may have found yourself on somewhat of an emotional rollercoaster, I hope that most importantly you know that you are NOT alone. I, and so many others, unite with you in your experiences, and we celebrate your ability to SURVIVE! I challenge you to continue to LIVE and as my friend Simona Lynch would say, to L.O.V.E.—Lead Other Victims Everyday—into hope and healing. You are powerful, courageous and undefeatable. On the days that you forget just how strong you are, encourage yourself with these life giving words from Gloria Gaynor: I will Survive. Oh as long as I know how to love, I know I'll stay alive. I've got all my life to live, and I've got all my love to give. And I'll survive. I will survive. Hey Hey!!

Sincerely,
A Survivor

Courtney N. Hauser, LPC

From Victim to Survivor

This was a Great Read!!

Made in the USA
Columbia, SC
28 January 2020

87251403R00089